MADAGASCAR
Island of the Ancestors

MADAGASCAR

Island of the Ancestors

JOHN MACK

Published for the
Trustees of the British Museum by
British Museum Publications Limited

© 1986, The Trustees of the British Museum
Published by British Museum Publications Ltd,
46 Bloomsbury Street, London WC1B 3QQ

British Library Cataloguing in Publication Data

Mack, John
    Madagascar: island of the ancestors.
    1. Ethnology—Madagascar   2. Madagascar—
    Social life and customs
    I. Title   II. British Museum. *Trustees*
    306′.0969′1   GN661.M2

    ISBN 0–7141–1580–0

Designed by Harry Green

Filmset in Photina and printed by
BAS Printers Limited, Over Wallop, Hampshire

Front cover: Sakalava man standing beside a figure suitably
armed with gun and spear at the entrance to a grave-site.

Back cover: Betsimisaraka woman weaving the raffia cloth
distinctive of eastern Madagascar on her single-heddle loom.

Page 1: Wood-carving of two birds in a pose derived from
images found on a Sakalava tomb. H. 90 cm. MAA 62–1–17.

Pages 2–3: Wood panel with animal and bird imagery.
Mahafaly. L. 105 cm. MAA 63–17–92.

The Trustees of the British Museum
gratefully acknowledge the support
and encouragement given to its work
in Madagascar by:

 **AIR MADAGASCAR**

                and

 The British Museum Society

ACKNOWLEDGEMENTS

All field photographs were taken by the author except
for the following: p. 29, Maurice Bloch;
p. 20, Brian Durrans; front cover, Jacques Hannebicque;
pp. 75, 78, 80, 87, Otto Peetz collection.
    Photographs of objects have been provided by the
British Museum's Photographic Service. Sources of
other illustrations are given at the end of their captions.
    Line drawings and maps are by Mina McElwain.

Contents

Preface

There are many reasons that might justify a major exhibition and an accompanying publication being devoted to a single country or a single culture. If a museum is fortunate enough to possess extensive and important holdings from one particular area, that would already be sufficient cause. However, the lack of resources as much as their abundance can also provide a viable motive, even if any associated fieldwork may be more prolonged and complex. There is, in consequence, the prospect of introducing a subject which is relatively little investigated, or known only to a few experts, and, it is hoped, of providing a stimulus to new and renewed interest.

In the case of Madagascar the collections housed in the British Museum have until recently been based very largely on donations from the families of missionaries, many of whom have maintained connections with the island over several generations. Although important in themselves such collections tend to reflect those regions in which the various British mission societies have been active and are unrepresentative of the island as a whole. The same situation is repeated throughout Great Britain: where ethnographic collections exist they rarely contain Malagasy material and, if they do, they are often exclusively from the more accessible, central parts of the island. Indeed apart from institutions in Madagascar itself, the other main historical collections are held in France and at the Field Museum in Chicago.

Both this introduction to the history and traditions of Madagascar and the exhibition to which it is intended as a guide seek to be as definitive as possible. It is written in the knowledge that the sources in English that might be available to the general reader are few and most of the relevant writing in French is not easily accessible. There remains much that could yet be said and done, and there are many subjects and regions of the island only touched on here that are capable of further discussion and development. As always in such circumstances the bibliography is not the least important section of this book. The library of the Museum of Mankind has sought in recent years to improve and increase its coverage of Madagascar, and thanks are due to the library staff for their many efforts in this direction.

The preparations for this handbook and exhibition, however, have not merely been conducted in London, nor has it been solely a British Museum project. From the outset the Malagasy authorities have given encourage-

6

ment and much practical help with the result that it has become a co-operative venture. For the Museum's part the first and most sustaining support has been that enthusiastically and generously given by the British Museum Society whose Chairman and Council have enabled me to undertake two periods of field research and collecting and supported preliminary visits by my colleague Brian Durrans. The British Council has also offered assistance in enabling Malagasy colleagues to become involved in preparations in London. Contributions towards the mounting of the exhibition have been received from E. D. and F. Man (Coffee) Ltd, Dalgety International Trading Ltd and Ove Arup Partnership. In Madagascar particular thanks are due to the staff of the Ministère de la Culture et de l'Art Révolutionnaires (MCAR) and to Air Madagascar whose participation has been of inestimable value. Many others have also helped at various stages of the work, amongst whom have been Maurice Bloch, Ben Bronson, Bob Dewar, Fulgence Fanony, Gillian Feeley-Harnik, Rev. J. T. Hardyman, Richard Hyde, Richard Langridge, Malcolm McBain, Malcolm McLeod, Eugène Mangalaza, Rakotomalala, Rasolofo, Alison Richards, Penelope Simon, Henry Wright and Pierre Vérin.

None of these, however, will I am sure feel slighted if the fullest acknowledgement here is reserved to the Director and staff of the Musée d'Art et d'Archéologie in Antananarivo. This institution has lent many of the major works in its care to make possible the fullest coverage of the island's artistic traditions in the exhibition, and Jean-Aimé Rakotoarisoa also appropriately contributes a foreword. He and his staff have gone further and shared the rigours of the fieldwork and collecting which have been the prelude to this exhibition and have assisted in mounting it. In particular, I should like to thank Ramilisonina, Ndriana Rajaobelison (MCAR) and Jean-Louis Raveloson, who have ensured that the whole process was rewarding and contributed much personally to its success.

JOHN MACK
Assistant Keeper, Museum of Mankind

Foreword

In 1973 the Musée d'Art et d'Archéologie (MAA) in association with the Musée d'Ethnographie in Neuchâtel, Switzerland, mounted an exhibition entitled 'Malgache, qui es-tu?' This drew heavily on the collections which the MAA, particularly in the preceding decade, had sought to assemble in order that Madagascar itself should retain representative collections of the heritage of its various peoples. This present publication introduces a second and major co-operative venture to which the joint resources of the MAA and, on this occasion, the British Museum have contributed. It is not merely, however, the outcome of adding together the collections available in two institutions and exhibiting the best of them. Rather it draws on a programme of fieldwork and research in which both museums have been engaged over a period of years concentrating on parts of the vast island that are most incompletely studied. This has been conducted under the auspices of the Malagasy Ministère de la Culture and the Université de Madagascar.

The title of the first exhibition in Switzerland already gives some indication of how little Madagascar and Malagasy (Malgache) culture were known beyond the context of the Indian Ocean some thirteen years ago. We were introducing Madagascar and also some of the problems faced by the disciplines concerned with the understanding of its cultures and their past. Of these archaeology perhaps was the most in its infancy. Indeed, since the peopling of the island has taken place, on most estimates, only within the last 1,500 years, the whole idea of an archaeology of Madagascar seemed to some Utopian. In fact the archaeology of the interior of Africa, although possessed of much greater time depth, fares still worse in terms of the availability of the archives, texts and historical documents against which to set archaeological findings. Here, however, in Sub-Saharan Africa, archaeology has developed and considerable advances have been made.

The historical sources concerning Madagascar are patchy but, where they exist, they are extremely rich. They are of three kinds. The first, and the most familiar tool of the historian, are accounts and reports written by outsiders, whether traders, missionaries or would-be settlers. Those by Europeans go back to the sixteenth century, although Madagascar is also recorded by a variety of Arab authors writing in earlier times. Madagascar as a name is generally attributed to the invention of Marco Polo who heard of the existence of the island from Arab traders. He may, indeed, have mis-heard it and confused the island with Mogadishu, an important trading centre in Somalia (Madagascar and Mogadishu are certainly sufficiently alike as names for this to be possible).

The other two kinds of written source are directly Malagasy in origin. One, discussed below by John Mack, is the Malagasy texts written in Arabic script (*Sorabe*) by peoples in the south-east of the island. The content of these texts is various but includes much historical information, as yet insufficiently studied. The other is the remarkable series of oral histories, dealing with Imerina in the centre of the island, which were written down and published in the second half of the nineteenth century by the Jesuit priest Père Callet (Callet 1873). Also noteworthy is the important Malagasy historian Raombana who was sent to England in 1820 to receive his education. He later returned to become an influential secretary to the Merina Queen Ranavalona I and left in his *History, Annals and Journal* a major document of the period written by a Malagasy in English. All of these local sources constitute an archive of the highest quality, although in terms of subject are effectively limited to the centre of the island and its south-eastern coastline.

These historical sources have also proved valuable to ethnographers, and, indeed, the same disparities between research in the centre of the island and amongst its coastal populations have characterised the ethnographic account. Outstanding interpretations of the traditions of the Merina in particular have been made. For some of the island's peoples, however, the only significant reports remain those of the nineteenth-century authors, and serious studies of the arts of many regions have yet to be undertaken.

Yet we are certainly in a better position now to answer the question 'Malgache qui es-tu?' than we were in the early 1970s, even if there remains much to be done. Furthermore, the question itself might now be approached in a rather different way than it was in the past. For a long time studies of Malagasy culture history tended to resolve themselves into questions of origins. The task of those disciplines concerned with the island's settlement and history frequently reverted to comparisons with what was known of other Indian Ocean peoples. Who the Malagasy were was a question of identifying which parts of Malagasy culture are of South-East Asian, Near Eastern or African derivation. These issues remain important. Increasingly, however, new questions and problems arise concerning developments within Madagascar itself, questions of its economic and agricultural development and of inter-regional relationships, of the impact of man on his environment, of the emergence of ethnic groups and state structures, and of the variety of processes involved on an island the size of Madagascar.

Within the last decade many of these questions have been posed by Malagasy themselves as a result of archaeological work, historical and ethnographic research in which they have been directly involved and which they have initiated. It is no longer a matter of using historical and ethnographic research to prove the accuracy of some written account or piece of received wisdom. There is much that remains to be discovered rather than simply verified. In this the MAA, as other Malagasy institutions, has sought to retain as broad and multi-disciplinary an approach as possible.

It is in this context and spirit that we have welcomed and participated in a joint programme of ethnographic research with the British Museum's Museum of Mankind. The exhibition which has resulted seeks to cover as much of Madagascar as possible and the publication John Mack has prepared draws on sources from many parts of the island. This attempt at a wider coverage of Malagasy tradition is possible only because in our field-work we have sought to concentrate on major areas and regions not previously investigated. In particular, research has been initiated in the inhospitable and sometimes hardly accessible areas of the eastern rainforests, and many of the objects and traditions recorded have not previously been studied. Toamasina (formerly Tamatave), the provincial capital in the middle of the coastline occupied by the Betsimisaraka peoples, had no centre for research in the historical sciences at the time this project began. Now, at least in part as a result of the work already undertaken there, it promises to emerge as an important regional centre of archaeological, historical and ethnographic or anthropological research. Beyond that, if as a result of the occasion afforded by this publication and exhibition we are able to introduce Madagascar, its peoples, cultures and arts to a wider international audience, then this joint project will have more than fulfilled its aims.

J-A. RAKOTOARISOA

Introduction

Islands – and especially those that have enjoyed a degree of isolation from outside influence – are the set pieces of scientific debate. Unaffected by external pressures they are free to evolve and develop their own distinctive characteristics. Such expectation was most famously celebrated in Darwin's observations on the variation of species in the Galapagos Archipelago; but the Galapagos are not uniquely privileged in this respect. Had the HMS *Beagle* voyaged in the western reaches of the Indian Ocean instead of round the southern extremities of the Americas, Madagascar might well have provided similar inspiration to scientific advancement. It remains a living museum of natural history to the point where, even outside professional circles, discussion of the oddities of its flora and fauna has sometimes threatened to overshadow interest in its peoples.

Certainly beyond its shores the names of its different types of lemur – the *aye-aye*, the *indri*, the *sifaka*, or the ring-tailed *maki* – may be more familiar than the names of any of its ethnic groups. Madagascar is home to over thirty species of this, the most primitive of the primates. It survives here and virtually nowhere else precisely because, having had no land connection to the mainland of Africa for many millions of years, the island lacks the animals of prey that have elsewhere contributed to the extinction of this earliest of the primates. The crocodile is the only serious predator found in Madagascar and in view of its restricted riverine habits is by no means a general threat. Nevertheless, human activity has had and continues to have its effects. It is already perhaps eight centuries since the giant *Aepyornis maximus*, which stood some 3 m in height, became extinct. No doubt more species of lemur have suffered a similar fate, the result in no small measure of man's extensive destruction of natural habitats and forest environments. In addition to the lemur curiosities such as the hedgehog-like tenrec, hunted in some places but respected (and therefore still common) in others, the numerous colourful chameleons, or the strange and exotic insects and birds make the island a unique natural sanctuary.

This proliferation of types of faunal life, however, is not just a question of Madagascar's isolation and a result of an unusual mix of naturally selected 'fit' species. By comparison with the Galapagos it is gigantic: two and a half times the size of Great Britain, 1,600 km in length and aligned along a roughly north/south axis, the variety of its physical and climatic features is startling, more so than that found in Greenland, New Guinea or Borneo,

The ring-tailed lemur, one of nearly forty species that have been discovered on the island and each unique to Madagascar. They vary from animals the size of children down to that of a mouse. From Ellis 1859, p. 438.

Viewing a rare skeleton of *Aepyornis maximus* in a Paris museum. The reconstructed bird was much fuller-bellied than this ostrich-like skeleton might suggest. Occasional finds of bones and eggs are still made. From *Antananarivo Annual*, 1896.

the only three island masses that are larger. Not only are unique varieties of tropical vegetation native and a greater range of orchids found here than anywhere else, but Madagascar also possesses divergent types of cacti adapted to quite different circumstances. The slight variations Darwin detected from island to island in the Galapagos are much more dramatic in Madagascar where no single climate or type of environment can be said to be characteristic.

The east coast receives the highest levels of rainfall, in places reaching averages in excess of 355 cm annually, and is especially prey to cyclones in the early months of the year. Here, along the narrow strip of land between the seaboard itself and a steep scarp face which separates the Indian Ocean coast from the central spine of the island, the main regions of luxuriant tropical forest occur. In many places this remains a near-impenetrable tangle, despite the fact that much of the forest is already second growth having originally been cut back and cleared for agricultural purposes. Where primary forest is still intact this is often for specific cultural reasons, frequently indicating the site of an ancestral burial-ground at which it is forbidden to clear the undergrowth. The ravenala, or traveller's tree, with its distinctive fan-shaped palm leaves and trunk from which pure water may be tapped, is familiar. Introduced crops such as vanilla, cloves, sugar-cane and coffee also thrive along this humid stretch of coastline.

By contrast with this rich tropical environment, the centre of the island, the so-called plateau, is at once cooler, drier (with only 127 cm of rain per year), and, most striking of all, is very substantially denuded. Within little more than 100 km from the coast vigorous growth has given way to a near treeless expanse of poor coarse grasslands and red lateritic soils. The change in climate is due largely to the increased elevation of the plateau which rises to about 1,300 m, although being far from flat it has considerable variations: the Ankaratra mountain range to the south of the capital Antananarivo has peaks in excess of 2,500 m. The changing appearance of the region, however, has another cause: it did once support forest vegetation; the lunar landscape of today is the direct result of the ubiquitous habit of systematically burning off the vegetation to facilitate rice cultivation, a practice known in Madagascar as *tavy*. Nowadays only outcrops of the imported eucalyptus tree significantly interrupt the acres of rolling prairie land.

Westwards and southwards from the central and more northerly parts of the island the climate gradually resumes tropical proportions, although increasing heat is matched by a relatively dry climate falling off in the south-west to as little as 5 cm of rain a year. Grasslands gradually give way to arid semi-desert conditions which prevail over substantial parts of the south. Here, too, in areas such as the Horombe plain the grass is burnt off as on the plateau. The purpose, however, is less the creation of rice fields than the encouragement to growth of new shoots of grass to support the large herds of cattle which are a predominant element in the traditional economy of the more southerly and westerly parts of the island. The baobab tree adds to the eccentricity of the vegetation which includes in more arid areas the unique tall spines of didierea and forests of cactus as impenetrable

A remoter part of the eastern rain forests where the forest cover has been substantially cleared for cultivation.

The central part of the island's plateau. The bare hillsides have been extensively terraced to take the forthcoming planting of the rice crop, and the valley bottom contains flatter paddy fields.

as the lush tropical vegetation of the east coast. Under French colonial rule insects were introduced that attacked these vast thickets of cactus in order to subjugate local peoples who would otherwise retreat within them and become inaccessible to would-be administration.

Clearly the same combination of an isolated position and a wide variety of differing ecological circumstances has implications for the cultural as well as the natural situation of Madagascar. The use of a single term, Malagasy, to refer to the island's people and its language may suggest uniformity, but in fact there is arguably as much cultural variation in Madagascar as there is diversity of climate, vegetation or wildlife. It has been suggested

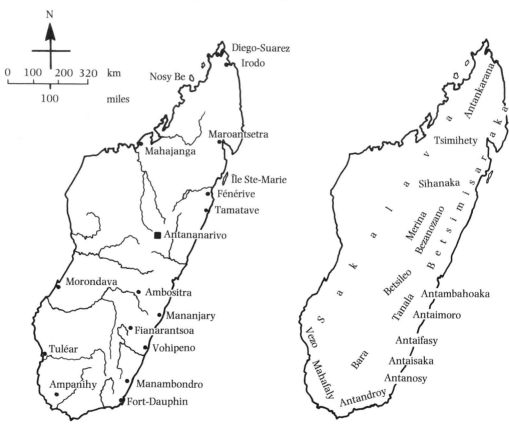

Madagascar.
Left Place-names.
Right Ethnic groups.

that the traditional livelihood of different regions may range between economies based in rice cultivation and more or less pure pastoralism. The inclusion of rice and cattle as major items of traditional trade between different regions has not led to any general levelling out of the Malagasy economy; each region retains its characteristic features.

What goes for the economy of the island also substantially holds for other aspects of cultural practice. Thus, although Malagasy is one language it has many divergent dialects. Merina, the language (and name) of the people occupying the area of the plateau around the capital, and the official language of state, is understood throughout the island. Local dialects, however, may in some cases be sufficiently divergent as to be virtually unintelligible one to another. Madagascar has eighteen officially recognised ethnic groups and yet within the larger, most notably amongst the Betsimisaraka of the east coast, there may already be a number of identifiable local dialects. With other aspects of Malagasy culture uniformity is also often more apparent than real, based more on its *dissimilarity* from ways of life familiar from the neighbouring African continent, or other point of comparison, than on its own internal consistency.

The dissimilarities from Africa are immediately apparent even to the most casual of observers. The island's international airport lies on the plateau. Here a very high proportion of the population are light-skinned, straight-haired, unmistakably Asian in appearance. Anyone conversant with Bantu languages – even with Swahili, the language of coastal peoples in eastern Africa and a major language of trade throughout the whole maritime region in the vicinity of northern Madagascar – will none the less find very small numbers of familiar words. At least 93 per cent of the basic Malagasy vocabulary is Malayo-Polynesian in origin, comparison with Batak, Javanese and Maanjan, a language spoken in central Borneo, having shown many common retentions. A taxi journey to Antananarivo can also be instructive. Signs which read 'City –7,000 francs, Marriages, Funerals and Exhumations – price negotiable' are not entirely apocryphal. Certainly the practice of second burial, and that of periodically removing the bones of the deceased from a tomb in order to rewrap them in a silk shroud, are well established in Madagascar. They do not occur so explicitly on adjacent parts of the African continent.

As it happens, some aspects of this picture need revising to take account of the situation beyond the plateau. Second burial and the 'turning' of the bones of the ancestors are by no means an inevitable feature of the Malagasy treatment of the dead; elsewhere there are quite different traditions. It should also be stressed that although people of Asian descent may be found throughout Madagascar African physical types are dominant beyond the plateau. In fact, taking the population as a whole, African characteristics are in the majority, which is much as might be expected. After all, Madagascar's isolation is not an absolute condition; what is effective insulation against invasive floral and faunal types from the African mainland may not prove an insuperable barrier to human enterprise. Madagascar is not Easter Island; it lies only 400 km from the African seaboard, sufficiently close for it to be a natural member of the Organisation of African Unity in modern times and to have developed significant relations with its continental neighbours. Furthermore, in more remote centuries domesticated animals, and particularly cattle, must have been shipped across to Madagascar in sufficient numbers for them to have become a major part of the economy and to have been present from the earliest times. The contacts back and forth must have been more extensive than the present cultural and linguistic priority of Asian traits would otherwise suggest.

In what follows an attempt has been made to sum up some of the more authoritative findings of archaeologists and historians, together with any additional observations that the study of anthropology and artefacts might have to offer. Much of the debate centres on the interplay of African and Asian features, and material objects in particular have often been invoked in support of one or other version of the cultural mix. The result is a tendency to unravel the fabric of Malagasy culture into what are presumed to be its likely constituent elements; however, where there is an African style of musical instrument on Madagascar, it does not follow that there is an African playing it. Similarly, it is notable that a type of canoe which uses the single outrigger survives only amongst the Vezo, a small group of people living in south-west Madagascar. Canoes of this type contrast with the standard African dug-out (which predominates elsewhere on the island) and are more familiar from Oceania or South-East Asia. Its presence in Madagascar is therefore evocative of one version of Malagasy origins; but it is worth noting that the Vezo are amongst the most divergent of the island's peoples. Their livelihood is more or less entirely based on fishing

Child completing a working model of a lorry in which to tow babies around the village. Betsimisaraka.

which elsewhere, even if it is practised, has nothing like the same over-riding importance. Furthermore, in other ways the Vezo are exceptional: they do not, for example, practise circumscision which is a central ritual elsewhere on the island, circumcision often being for men a crucial condition of access to ancestral tombs. This in itself argues for a strong African rather than South-East Asian element in Vezo culture, and to this day they retain strong contacts with coastal peoples in Mozambique.

Instead of breaking Malagasy culture down into various historical components, the intention here will be to assemble it. The title of this book and of the exhibition it accompanies – *Madagascar, Island of the Ancestors* – has a double reference. On the one hand it draws attention to these questions of Malagasy origins and subsequent historical developments. Much of the discussion involves reference to events taking place beyond the shores of Madagascar itself. Indeed, the major question which arises – the process by which Malagasy culture achieved so comprehensive an overlay of Asian features when over half of its population, on the basis of physical and other evidence, are of African background – remains unanswered. This can only really be tackled by a consideration of matters internal to Madagascar; archaeologists, many of them Malagasy, are beginning to look at these issues. The first section of the book will consider the better-documented developments of Malagasy history – the building into Malagasy culture of Islamic elements, the evolution of states, and latterly the influence of European culture, especially the impact of missionary activity.

The second reference implied in the title is to that body of tradition which regulates Malagasy life up to the present day. 'Tradition' in Malagasy is *fomban-drazana*, literally the ways of the ancestors, or ancestral practice. The allusion to the community of the ancestors is significant. Indeed, if a single characteristic can be said to draw together the diverse cultural practice of Madagascar, it is the constant invoking of the ancestors and ancestral practice as the first and most significant point of reference. The final section of the book will consider the ancestral monuments, tombs and cenotaphs, principal artefacts in Malagasy culture and the scenes of many of the central events in Malagasy life. Despite the modern judicial system, exclusion from the ancestral burial-place, the traditional penalty for the most serious offences against the community, remains the ultimate of sanctions. Yet it is not just in funerary practice that the relationship of the living and the dead is at issue; it pervades all aspects of Malagasy life.

PART 1

The ancestors

Early settlers

Outrigger canoe as used and photographed among the Vezo in south-western Madagascar. Here they continue to be used in fishing, although the original ocean-going versions could have been considerably larger.

Speculations about such fundamental matters as who the first settlers in Madagascar were, precisely when they arrived, where they came from, what parts of the island they initially occupied, what language they spoke, or indeed what more general cultural characteristics they possessed, have so far failed to resolve themselves into any totally compelling consensus. No firm archaeological evidence of what is likely to be the earliest human occupation has yet been recovered and perhaps never will be. Some versions of Malagasy prehistory are fuller than others positing approximate chronologies and seeking to identify probable cultural origins and routes followed by presumed waves of migrants. Yet it remains difficult to give a detailed and measured account particularly of the earliest phases of the island's occupation. The most accessible attempt at an overall view available in English is to be found in Brown 1978, although other evidence has come to light since the research on which this account is based was conducted.

A convenient watershed in the consideration of Malagasy prehistory lies in a period between about the ninth and eleventh centuries AD. By this time Madagascar was widely settled, albeit by dispersed communities with relatively limited contacts and living in quite different circumstances. Irodo, a site lying on the north-east coast, flourished from possibly as early as the ninth until the sixteenth century, being home to a population who gathered large amounts of shellfish and may have exploited the surrounding hillsides for agricultural purposes. In the south at the same time the coastal region was known to fishermen living probably much as the Vezo of today, while the arid interior was beginning to be penetrated by cattle-keepers. Trade, possibly from Madagascar as well as to it, was established and the island was in the process of being embraced by the tide of Arabico-Swahili peoples who spread through the western parts of the Indian Ocean from the beginning of the present millennium, and whose presence and passage are extensively documented up and down the East African coast.

Irodo, and similar sites dated to this period, are clearly not the first communities to establish themselves on the island. There must have been significant occupation before that date. Even so the first feet would seem to have been set on Madagascar within, and possibly well within, the first millennium. AD 500 is often quoted as a likely date for the event, although historical linguistics, as yet unverified by any other form of firm evidence,

Pages 18–19 The Malagasy bellows, used in tandem for smelting and singly for smithing. Iron is no longer smelted in Madagascar, but blacksmiths continue with the same essentially South-East Asian technology in manufacturing agricultural and domestic implements. From Ellis 1859, p. 264.

Madagascar and the Indian Ocean.

point to slightly earlier dates. None the less, this is already some way into the Christian era, and very recent even in terms of the peopling of other more remote islands and geographical outposts such as those in the Pacific.

The game of guessing at the identity of these first settlers has proved endlessly fascinating. Some have suggested that amongst the candidates must be South-East Asian mariners carried directly by the prevailing winds and currents across the vast expanses of the Indian Ocean, a distance of some 6,400 km from Indonesia. A Kon Tiki style expedition, sailing a suitably constructed outrigger canoe, has even sought to test the possibility, taking forty-nine days to make the crossing. In the end, however, accidental discovery in this way cannot have been a method of significantly peopling the island. However plausible the journey in one direction may or may not be proved to be, not only would it be necessary to accept that such voyages were successfully repeated but the fact that intervening islands – Réunion and Mauritius – were found to be unoccupied before Europeans arrived would need to be explained away. Still more improbable is a suggestion the pioneers were Buddhist monks.

Settlement by way of the East African coast is by far the likeliest scenario. Authority is available for a thoroughly South-East Asian element amongst

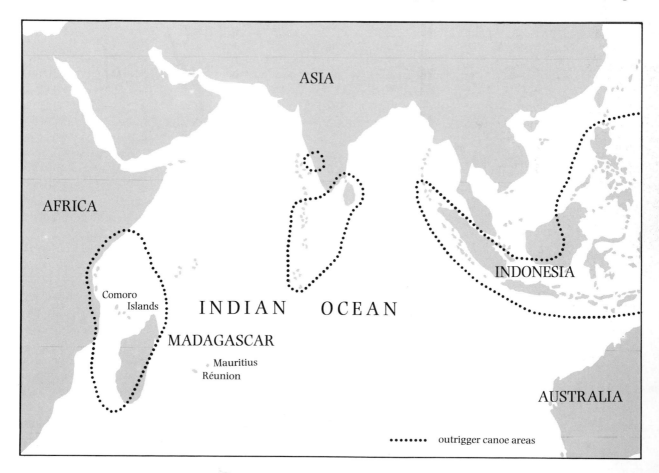

ASIA

AFRICA

INDONESIA

Comoro
Islands

INDIAN   OCEAN

MADAGASCAR

Mauritius
Réunion

AUSTRALIA

••••••• outrigger canoe areas

these and subsequent settlers (Grandidier 1908) and for a substantial African impact (Ferrand 1908). However, more recent versions of Malagasy prehistory have all favoured some form of coming together of African and Asian populations as the essential theme of the story, making Madagascar home to the only truly cosmopolitan culture of this kind anywhere (Deschamps 1960, Kent 1970, Vérin 1975, Brown 1978). Certainly the evidence of physical anthropology lends itself very readily to an account that acknowledges the joint heritage of the Malagasy. Debate has thus moved from backing exclusively one or other of the available models to trying to establish where and when some form of symbiosis took place.

Whichever view is taken, however, it must be capable of accounting for two sets of facts. One is the question of language: Malagasy, as noted in the Introduction, is a Malayo-Polynesian language with close affinities to languages spoken to the present day in Indonesia. It is relatively homogeneous with no markedly greater proportion of Bantu, and thus African, terms from one dialect to another. The sole exception is the speech of some parts of the north-west coast where more recent contacts with Swahili-speaking traders have led to additional borrowings. Otherwise the number of Bantu words is both in proportion and remarkably small.

The Malagasy language

For this situation to have arisen a Malayo-Polynesian element must have been prominent in the earliest phases of the island's occupation. The suggestion that a later conquest by an already established population would produce this same result in terms of the relative uniformity of language is discounted for a number of reasons. Firstly there is no other evidence of such a conquest from outside the island. Equally only two successful indigenous attempts at empire-building, the development of kingdoms among the Sakalava and the Merina in historical times, if much more than local events, were still far from all-embracing. While Sakalava domination may account for the disappearance of small communities speaking diverse languages reported along the west coast, neither this nor Merina expansion is adequate explanation for the larger eradication of speech communities that would otherwise have to be envisaged. In any case, there is plenty of evidence from elsewhere in the world to show that conquerors often adopt the speech of the conquered rather than the other way round (Southall 1975). Either way the same conclusion is arrived at, that Malagasy, with its roots in the languages of South-East Asia, was from the start the only tongue spoken throughout the island, whatever language smaller dispersed settlers might have retained for a period as their original speech.

It should not be forgotten, however, that small as the Bantu element in Malagasy is it is still there; and it is not a regional feature but common in all the various dialects. In particular, terms associated with animal husbandry are clearly derived from Bantu words – *omby* ('ox') *akoho* ('hen'), or *akanga* ('guinea-fowl'), for instance. The phonetics of Malagasy confirm this early Bantu influence, and the fact that, again, these are island-wide features of the language suggests they have been there virtually from the start.

In view of all this, current debate envisages a wave of migrants passing round the northern fringes of the Indian Ocean, possibly taking in southern India itself, Sri Lanka and the Maldives, before moving into its western extremities and touching on the East African coast during the early part of the first millennium AD. It was these migrants, ultimately of South-East Asian origin, who were to occupy Madagascar in significant numbers and for whom this may have been their journey's end. What remains unclear is the character of their relationship to African populations. A number of possibilities have been canvassed. A period of settlement on the African mainland prior to arrival on the island is clearly quite likely. Similarly, it has been suggested that Madagascar may have been used as a base from which these migrating peoples explored the lands lying on the other side of the Mozambique channel. The fact that large fleets of Betsimisaraka and Sakalava raiders ravaged wide areas of the East African coast and intervening islands to the north-west of Madagascar in the late eighteenth and early nineteenth centuries affirms at least the possibility of such exploitation of the mainland from which an acquaintance with African cultures might derive. Increasingly, the Comores have been identified as an important stepping-stone between continental Africa and its largest off-shore island.

Material culture

The track followed by South-East Asian migrants is quite clearly perceptible – it is witnessed in the distribution of their means of transport, the outrigger canoe. It is such details in the field of ethnography which provide the second set of data that needs to be accommodated within the schemes proposed by more directly historical disciplines. The presence of the outrigger canoe in Madagascar – the emblem of South-East Asian culture, is in practice problematical, not to say paradoxical, being associated with one of the most divergent of the island's peoples, the Vezo. The dangers of isolating out individual features of a cultural assemblage for separate treatment, let alone of endowing them with historical significance in default of other kinds of more convincing evidence, are clear enough.

Deschamps, as a preamble to his detailed account of Malagasy history, sought (1961, pp. 21–3) to tabulate aspects of Malagasy cultural practice according to their presumed places of origin. Some of these are certainly definitive – the presence of exclusively rectangular architecture (as opposed to round huts), for instance, or the use in ironworking of a form of bellows employing a system of pistons are clearly Indonesian features. Yet the nearest approach to a properly constructed analysis of Malagasy artefacts concerns musical instruments (Sachs 1938). Here the various classes of instruments have been fully described in terms of their cultural origin such as the tube zither (*valiha*) of South-East Asian derivation or the calabash-resonated cordophone (*jejolava*) of African. Instruments of Arab origin, the flute, for example, are seen as later acquisitions. What is missing from the account, however, is some discussion of the music played on the various instruments, of the occasions to which particular instruments or music are appropriate, the content of songs, associated dance movement and other parts of the complex within which the musical instrument is

Typical Malagasy rectangular housing in the Antaimoro region in the southeast of the island. The set of the roof and gable is reminiscent of Oceanic architecture with no obvious African parallel.

Elaborate *valiha*, here strung with metallic cord. A more rudimentary version is simply a tube of bamboo from which splints are raised along its length. L. 74 cm. MAA N/N.

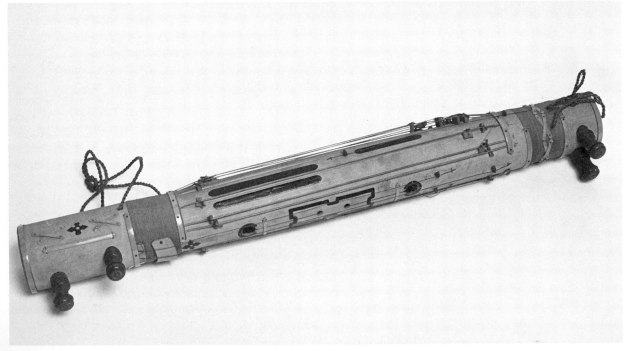

Above Playing the cordophone which uses the calabash resonator, an instrument also extensively found on adjacent parts of the African continent. The painter, Rainimaharosoa, was a mission-trained artisan who died in 1926. Most of his work dates, however, from the opening decade of the century.

Above right A *valiha* player painted by the same artist.

culturally located. Even if the language used in singing a song is Malayo-Polynesian, the rhythm may not be. Similarly, an African instrument may play an Indonesian tune, and vice versa. During fieldwork in eastern Madagascar, for example, the playing of the accordion, even in the remotest villages, was found to be commonplace; it had very largely replaced more traditional Malagasy instruments. If the instrument was of European derivation, however, the music played upon it was certainly not; it remained entirely traditional with a strong South-East Asian element.

Arguably weaving is the most important element in the material complex. Deschamps mentions the weaving of cotton both as an Indonesian and an African trait. Beyond that it is possible to distinguish different influences in the technology of Malagasy looms, and to say something about the affinities of different patterns applied to cloth. Most significant, however, is the use of the finished textile which through its association with mortuary practice in a number of parts of the island forms part of a crucial complex of cultural activity.

There are three basic types of fibre woven in Madagascar. Cotton and silk are both traditional in the plateau area and produced and spun locally. They are the main raw materials used by Merina and Betsileo weavers and either may appropriately be woven to produce a burial shroud (*lamba mena*), although silk is much the more prestigious fibre. The other common type of Malagasy textile is raffia cloth. This is prepared from the stripped membranes of the raffia palm split into thin lengths and neatly joined together to give continuous warp and weft elements to be mounted on the loom. The result is a supple cloth that can be comfortably worn as clothing. Nowadays the main centres of raffia weaving are found amongst the Betsimisaraka in the eastern forests, although here it is not the custom to use woven cloth to wrap up a corpse. Traditionally raffia was also woven amongst the Sakalava in the west, a practice which has foundered in recent years and is now difficult to find. Raffia may also be mixed with other fibres to produce different effects, with cotton, for instance, to give a very fine cloth or, in modern times, with long strips of rag to give a thick blanket.

In addition to these, two more unexpected weaving fibres may be mentioned. One is bark, which is used for weaving cloth amongst the Zafimaniry, a small forest community who may well have had a more considerable effect on the arts of Madagascar than their past obscurity might otherwise suggest. (The southern Betsileo also once used it.) There is sometimes confusion between barkcloth, that is, bark which is beaten out with a mallet and felted, and the process of retting, soaking the bark to separate out the longitudinal fibres which may subsequently be woven on a loom. The Zafimaniry in fact do both, although it is the woven bark which is their speciality and which is used, again, as burial cloth. The weaving of banana fibre is also reported in this area.

Finally, woollen cloth is produced in southern Madagascar. The centre is at Ampanihy in Mahafaly country, and the raw material is goat's wool. This, however, is not the basis of a traditional textile industry but has developed during the colonial era as a commercial venture. Cotton is the more familiar fibre used in weaving not only among the Mahafaly but also their neighbours, the Antandroy.

At present the only type of traditional loom which is certainly still in use on the island is that which employs the single heddle. The double heddle loom which, although a more complex structure, has certain advantages in enabling design to be incorporated into cloth did certainly exist in the past. Its use is well-authenticated for the Maroantsetra region (Molet 1952), and during fieldwork among the Betsimisaraka it was accurately described on a number of occasions by people who had seen or heard of such a device in use further to the north. Sometimes it was identified as Tsimihety, although the possibility that it was once more widely distributed in the urban centres of the north of the island cannot be dismissed; it may indeed still exist in some parts.

However, all the remaining looms share the same distinctive feature: each uses what is called a fixed heddle – that is to say, the heddle stick is held in position throughout the process of weaving, and shed and countershed are effected simply by manipulating the shed stick. The heddle may be supported in one of two ways. Firstly, it may be placed on some form of stand erected at either side of the loom itself which is laid out horizontally. This feature is typically that of southern Madagascar, and of the Betsileo and the Merina in the plateau area. Generally it has been assumed to be the only form of loom found on the island, and its distribution has been used to associate Madagascar with weaving technologies in Eastern Africa and through into the Sahara and Mediterranean areas. Ling Roth (1917, p. 48), indeed, in a classic early study regards it as having been diffused from Madagascar.

There is, however, another system of fixing the heddle which is used

Betsileo woman weaving a man's cotton loin-cloth (*salaka*). Her loom incorporates the two stands on which the single heddle is supported.

Tsimihety woman using the typical loom of eastern Madagascar. Here the heddle is lashed to the rafters of the weaving hut. Pressing down with a loose stick opens up the two sets of warp elements. The cloth being woven is, as throughout eastern Madagascar, raffia.

on the island. This is the practice of lashing the heddle to the roof beams of a house or other structure within which weaving is to take place, and it is the method used in eastern Madagascar and found today most readily amongst the Betsimisaraka. This is a technique more typical of the Near East and documented best from the Yemen (Weir 1976), although in practice it is not a great technological jump from supporting the heddle on a stand to suspending it, and some East African looms come close to making that leap. What is perhaps indicative that there is a significant cultural and historical watershed between eastern Madagascar and elsewhere, however, is the fact that the cloth woven here is different, and the purposes to which it is put diverge.

On the plateau and down into southern Madagascar cloth typically includes weft patterning. This may be simply a limited pattern applied along its borders either as a woven design or even picked out in silver, lead or glass beads, or it may be richly decorated. The use of such weft patterning is one of the features of burial cloth. Along the east coast, however, all cloth is simply striped – there is no tradition of more elaborate geometric weft patterning. Furthermore, cloth is not generally found as an artefact of burial, nor is there a significant tradition of second burial which is a special characteristic of the funerary practice of the plateau areas. This form of the fixed heddle loom does seem to be associated with other cultural features which distinguish the practice of the eastern populations from other parts of the island – an indication of a still evident and separable influence in Malagasy culture. Some parts of the eastern coastline were more extensively settled by Islamised, if not actually Islamic, peoples during the present millennium. Some connection of loom technologies with the Near East is thus consistent with other historical data.

Example of weft-patterned silk textile. Although a burial cloth, this one is not of sufficient dimensions to envelop the corpse. Merina. 83 × 79 cm. BM 1969.Af14.2.

Zafimaniry woman weaving bast cloth on the backstrap loom. The wooden backrest is here covered for comfort. Usually, however, they are elaborately decorated with the geometric incised motifs characteristic of Zafimaniry wood-carving.

This, however, seems to suggest that any definitive signs of South-East Asian characteristics in Malagasy textile traditions have now been over-shadowed by subsequent developments beyond the point of recovery. Linguistic evidence might help root out further evidence but, while a proper investigation is yet to be made, many of the terms for weaving in Malagasy appear to be descriptive rather than technical; the use of a Malayo-Polynesian vocabulary is thus neither necessarily significant nor surprising. In practice Indonesian weaving technologies, like other aspects of a highly complex culture, are themselves various. Ling Roth (1917, p. 64) identifies three convergent weaving traditions which may represent a merging of historical cultures whose more precise origins and, more importantly, whose relative chronologies in the area remain obscure. Making relevant comparisons between evolving technologies at equivalent and significant historical moments is impractical. Two highly localised features of Malagasy weaving do, however, appear to be firmly evocative of South-East and Southern Asia.

One is concerned with the construction of the loom itself. This is the use of the so-called backstrap. Here, instead of the loom being held rigid by being tied to a fixed structure of some kind, it is the weight of the weaver's body pulling the loom towards her which alone tensions the warp threads. One end of the loom is held firm, tied usually to the inside of a hut wall at about chest height. The weaver sits on the ground and leans back against a rest which is itself tied to the loom directly in front of her. This draws the loom into tension to enable weaving to proceed. Once again, it is uniquely the Zafimaniry who employ this method in Madagascar; such a method of tensioning the warp is unknown in Africa.

A second undoubtedly Asian feature is the production of *ikat*-dyed cloth

Detail of an *ikat*-dyed raffia textile. Depending on size, such cloth might have been used as an awning, a mosquito net or as a burial shroud. Sakalava. MAA 71–2–28.

in several Sakalava areas to the south of the town of Mahajanga in western Madagascar. This tradition had virtually died out in the early 1970s (Heurtebize and Rakotoarisoa 1974) and was already on the wane when Linton collected there in 1926-7 for the Field Museum in Chicago. The procedure here is to dye the warp threads in advance of weaving, establishing the patterns which will ultimately appear on the woven cloth. The effect is often highly elaborate and dramatic. The technique is one with a very limited distribution in Africa, and it is rather to South and South-East Asia that one must look for any comparable and related tradition.

Datable textile remnants are yet to be recovered by archaeologists to confirm these remarks. So far all that has been found are quantities of spindle whorls indicating that cotton and probably silk have been woven in Madagascar for a considerable time. It would in particular be interesting to know if textiles regularly formed part of grave-goods in earlier periods. If so, this may add tentative support to the view that the practice of second burial in Madagascar is of some antiquity. Like the Malagasy language, second burial seems to be a direct cultural link with South-East Asia. Second burial is the custom whereby the deceased is buried shortly after death, perhaps in an improvised grave, to be exhumed once the flesh has left the body.

The bones are subsequently wrapped, preferably in a silk shroud, and placed in a family tomb alongside the bones of the ancestors of the kin group. Madagascar and Indonesia are the classic homes of the phenomenon for here they occur in striking form. The Merina, in addition, periodically remove the bones of the dead, carry them in procession, dance with them and wrap them in fresh shrouds before they are returned to the ancestral tombs (Bloch 1971, p. 138ff.). The ceremony is known in Malagasy as *famadihana*. This and other aspects of funerary practice are discussed in Part 2.

Board for playing *katra*, the Malagasy version of the game known in Africa as *mancala*, amongst other names. The four rows of holes duplicated the form of the board as found in East Africa. Sakalava. L. 65 cm. MAA 62–7–51.

In contemporary times textiles are nearly always associated with these events. Weaving, indeed, is even in some degree periodic in much of Madagascar with the more elaborate and expensive shrouds being produced to meet the demand which comes in the latter part of the year, the 'dry' season, when second burial, or *famadihana*, takes place. This, of course, is not to suggest that textiles in graves indicate second burial. Among the Sakalava, for instance, funerary shrouds of cloth are traditional, but second burial is not a visible cultural feature as it is elsewhere. Nevertheless, burial practice and weaving traditions are so closely connected that where the demand for cloth as clothing has disappeared with the advent of manufactured alternatives the demand for prestigious burial shrouds remains, ensuring a strong tradition of weaving.

Islam and astrology

Opposite A sacrificial animal, its head facing the east. The essential invocation to the ancestors is being made prior to the sacrifice itself. Bezanozano.

Into the present millennium Madagascar began to have its first sustained and significant contacts with the Islamised world. The island was in touch with trading communities on the Comoro archipelago and beyond to the developing town-states which grew up along the length of Africa's Swahili coast from Somalia to Mozambique. In each of these the evidence for a widespread adoption of Islamic faith and institutions is clear and undeniable. Excavation consistently reveals the establishment by the twelfth century of towns with characteristic mosques. Madagascar certainly had equivalent communities. The first stone-built mosque on the island seems to date from the thirteenth century and is from the site of

Remains of an Arab site in the Bay of Boina, north-western Madagascar. From Grandidier 1908, p. 162.

Mahilaka in the north. These developments were associated with the beginnings of larger areas of settlement and increasing populations. Mahilaka, for instance, grew to cover an area ten times larger than Irodo with its small clusters of households. Fortifications were erected and reliable wells established to provide for the growing numbers of people. Madagascar participated in long-distance networks of trade and exchange which brought high-quality Chinese wares and Near Eastern sgraffito bowls to the island, not just to its developing coastal centres but even to inland groups of cattle-herders in the south. In return Madagascar traded three-legged stone bowls, carved in chlorito-schist, and possibly other local products, while in the south pastoralists no doubt relied on surpluses of animal produce as the basis of exchange relationships.

Important ruler of the trading communities at Nosy Be, a small island adjacent to the north-western coast of Madagascar. His sword and attire associate him more directly than other Malagasy to the Islamised Swahili peoples of the East African coast. From H. Johnson, p. 440.

Traditional Betsimisaraka healer (*ombiasy*) with, before him, the various roots, twigs, leaves and cartridge case used as medical remedies. The bowl of water is used for mixing up the appropriate medicine. The dark seeds are used in divination.

There is, however, a paradox in all this. In the Comores and along the East African coast Islam remained the guiding theology, as it still is today; in Madagascar, however, Islamic communities in the full sense disappeared, whether by absorption, emigration or even eradication by the Portuguese in the sixteenth century. Practising Muslims in Madagascar are today effectively limited to much more recent settlements of Comorians and Shiite Muslims from India. Yet despite the fact that earlier Islamic communities were not sustained, aspects of Islamic culture, if not Islam itself, are now thoroughly established and pervasive features of Malagasy life. Indeed, the penetration of at least some Islamic-inspired notions has perhaps been more thoroughgoing in Madagascar, for these are embedded in Malagasy culture as a whole and not limited to the areas of original coastal settlement, as has largely been the case in many parts of East Africa.

In contemporary times there are two areas peopled by traditional Malagasy groups who would continue to identify themselves as *Silamo* (Islamic). These are at opposite ends of the island, in the north-west and the south-east. Indeed, it may well be that they are heirs to two entirely separate communities of settlement with independent associations to the Islamic world. Neither is today Islamic in the fuller religious and cultural sense. In the north Malagasy speech is laced with considerably higher proportions of Swahili and Arabic words than elsewhere. Elements of the Koran and of Islamic law are familiar. In the south-east, however, acquaintance with the Koran is minimal, and the tenets of the Islamic faith are known, if at all, only at second hand. Some recognisable Arabic terms and formulas are in use amongst ritual specialists and the elements of an alternative vocabulary based in Arabic are known to some members of aristocratic clans.

Yet, in spite of this, Islamic styles and fashions, some though by no means all of recent origin, are very evident in the south-east, amongst the Antambahoaka and especially the Antaimoro. Here the turban and the fez are worn together with versions of Arab robes whether a form of wrap-around garment or simply a white cotton coat. Moustaches trimmed in a style associated with Muslims are fashionable; and in at least one case, in the region of Vohipeno, mosque-like domes have been erected, not, however, at places of prayer but rather over graves. The graves also sometimes retain another and most un-Islamic feature – sculpted figurative grave-markers. It is especially the Anakara, the aristocratic groups, who have adopted these fashions, perhaps in response to the erosion in modern times of their former position of undisputed authority within what was once virtually a local caste system. They continue to emphasise their separateness by emphasising their Muslim connections.

Sorabe and scribes

What makes this feasible, in the absence of traditions of Koranic scholarship, is their possession of one unequivocal affirmation of their historic contact with the Islamic world. This is their ownership of sacred manuscripts known as *Sorabe* ('great writings'). These are found to this day amongst the Antaimoro and Antambahoaka and no doubt existed in the past

Antaimoro *mpanjaka*, *katibo* and clan leaders. The range of Islamic-inspired and other fashions familiar from the south-east of the island are evident.

Wood sculpture placed alongside an Antaimoro grave, 'dressed' with clothing of the recently deceased. The use of such imagery indicates the remove at which the Antaimoro stand from conventional Islam.

amongst other groups to the south, in particular amongst the Antanosy whose ruling lineage, the Zafy-Raminia, are related to the Antambahoaka. The paper on which they are written is produced locally (from beaten bark) as is the ink; the traditional pen is simply a shaped splint of bamboo. The texts are in Malagasy, but the script in which they are written is Arabic. Many examples of these texts still exist, often bound up in book form and carefully preserved within a continuing tradition of local scholarship. About twenty scribes are trained in each generation to read and to write in this unique script, both copying older manuscripts which, being preserved by being hung beneath the roof of a house, are somewhat at risk, and adding fresh texts to the traditional holdings. Few of these books would seem to date from much earlier than the mid-nineteenth century, although they may well be copies of much older manuscripts. Certainly examples held in European archives have been dated to the sixteenth century.

The books themselves are regarded as in some sense sacred. A greater part of their content certainly appears to be of a magico-religious character including tracts on such subjects as divination, astrology, medicine, amulets and geomancy. Others are more directly historical in substance, chronicling the traditional history of the aristocratic clans, recounting internal struggles and even in later documents noting aspects of British and French relations with Madagascar. That knowledge of *Sorabe* carries with it implications beyond those of mere historical or cabbalistic scholarship is also evident in the broader range of activities in which *katibo*, aristocratic scribes, specialise.

Perhaps the most celebrated historical account of the breadth of the activities of the *katibo* concerns an incident which took place in the early seventeenth century near Fort Dauphin, at that time a garrison held by the earliest of the French settlers to try and establish a base in Madagascar. Fort Dauphin (now Tolanaro) lies in the country of the Antanosy southwards from the main areas of Antaimoro settlement. The Antaimoro, how-

Antaimoro tombs with mosque-like structure for shelter, and cement human and humped cattle imagery on the roof. The tombs themselves are trenches cut into the floor. Details of the date of completion (1963) are written out in Roman and Arabic script using the Arab-derived calendar.

Example of *Sorabe* preserved by an Antaimoro *katibo* and photographed in the village where it, as numerous other 'great writings', are kept and consulted.

ever, exercised a considerable influence here some distance away by virtue of the essentially magical powers attributed to them in connection with their command of writing. It is recorded (by Flacourt, the French governor, in 1661, p. 171) that:

> These ombiasses are very feared, not just by the people, who regard them as sorcerers, but by their leaders [Antanosy chiefs] who employed them against

Basketry hat with red squares of thread
in imitation of Islamic fashions.
Antaimoro. H. 10 cm.
BM 1985.Af17.107.

the French. . . . They [the ombiasses] sent to the French fort baskets full of
papers with writing, eggs laid on Fridays covered with written symbols and
script, unbaked clay pots with inscriptions both inside and out, small coffins,
dugout canoes, paddles . . . all covered with inscribed signs, scissors and tongs.
. . . All of the ombiasses here are instructed by those from the land of Matetane.

The 'land of Matetane' is Matitana, an Antaimoro centre. *Ombiasses* are
ombiasy, a generic term in Malagasy which can refer to those who practise
the arts of divination, astrology or healing. Here the emphasis on writing
associates *katibo* with the sending of what are clearly missives of ill fortune.
Friday, for instance, is a powerful day (*andro mahery*) in Malagasy conception, a day when the strong would readily make a show of might before
the weak, and hence a day associated with bloodshed and death. To send
an egg laid on Friday is to send the things of Friday. Unbaked clay pots
are fragile, inadequate vessels in which to cook food or store liquids and
thus incapable of giving sustenance. Small coffins were a traditional charm,
examples having been documented from the Bara amongst other peoples,
who carried them to assure victory believing that they embodied the idea
that an enemy might die.

The most striking feature of this account is the fact that all these charms
and magical devices, whether or not actually constructed of paper, are
covered with inscriptions and writing. This is somewhat reminiscent of the
Muslim practice of carrying verses from the Koran often encased in a leather

pouch as a protective talisman, though here expanded to other materials and displayed, not hidden. We do not know the words or sense of the script received by the luckless French colonisers or, indeed, if the script was in Arabic or Malagasy. The significant fact, however, is that in the non-Islamic, non-literate cultures with which the Antaimoro came into contact writing itself had a powerful magical significance. The same in some degree holds today when, although Roman script has been introduced and literacy rates are in some areas remarkably high, an ability to use Arabico-Malagasy script remains limited to a very few. It could be argued that it is not simply the content of the *Sorabe* writings which give these books their special religious or magical significance, but the writing. From their mastery of script, and control over who should have access to its secrets, the *katibo* acquired for themselves immense power and influence.

The Islamised populations of the north-west have no manuscripts of the uniqueness or antiquity of the tradition of *Sorabe*, nor do they have a scribal aristocracy with the range of prestigious functions of the *katibo*. These and other variations between the two regions already suggest that the two traditions are separable and not merely fragmentary sections of a once-unified population. All of this adds credence to the Antaimoros' own account of their origin which would place their arrival in the south-east to about the fifteenth century, a period considerably after the first contacts and settlement which sustained and nurtured an Islamic community in the north of the island. The tradition of migration mentions a short period of settlement in the north-east but not of sufficient duration for the cohesion and identity of these migrating clans to be impaired. It seems clear enough that the Islamised populations who included the Antaimoro and the Antamba-hoaka were amongst the last peoples to arrive from outside the island before its discovery by the Portuguese in 1500 and the independent documentation which began to build up from that date.

Where they may have come from remains an open question. An ultimate connection with the Arabian peninsula has been suggested often enough, and certainly the similarity already noted between the Yemini loom and that found in eastern Madagascar is consistent with some historical contact with groups of people from that area. In addition the script used in writing *Sorabe* has been tentatively compared to Yemini forms. Another suggestion identifies them with a population known as Temur who appear to have disappeared from south-eastern Ethiopia at the relevant time (Kent 1970, p. 111). However, they do not at any rate seem to be part of the general interaction of Swahili peoples along the East African coast which kept the north-west of the island in contact with Islamic culture even after Islamic worship had otherwise ceased. Furthermore, in settling in south-eastern Madagascar they effectively isolated themselves from such cultural currents. Whether on arrival in Madagascar they were an already divergent Islamic sect, as has been proposed, or whether they were simply absorbed into Malagasy culture within a very few decades might be speculated upon. Certainly if they arrived in the fifteenth century with an Arabic language and script, they very rapidly adapted to local linguistic conditions, for there appear to be no examples of *Sorabe* which are written in Arabic. Equally

Wood-carving showing a consultation with a diviner, here using the *sikidy* system which employs seeds. Mahafaly. L. 50 cm. MAA 71–3–4.

no mosques or other forms of identifiable Islamic architecture are known from the area or have been located archaeologically.

However, Malagasy culture as a whole shows evidence of having been very thoroughly infiltrated by broader aspects of Islamic culture. In particular the practice of divination and the significance attached in Madagascar to different orientations can be related to Muslim inspiration and pervade the island's diverse peoples regardless of whether or not they can in any other fashion be shown to have some direct contact with the wider Islamic world. There is an obvious temptation to associate the activity of the Antaimoro with the spread of these features to other peoples on the island. *Katibo* were far from single-minded in their choice of clientele. Even Flacourt, the French governor of Fort Dauphin, was himself taught to read and translate Arabico-Malagasy texts. He was not alone. *Katibo* were active at the court of Andrianampoinimerina and influential in the development of the Merina state of which he was the founder. A school was established at Antananarivo at the beginning of the nineteenth century and some of the affairs of state administration began to be conducted in Arabic script. More generally the Antaimoro supplied the ruling clan amongst the Tanala and are sometimes associated with the founding of chiefdoms in Betsileo country in the southern parts of the plateau and in the south-west of the island. Itinerant Antaimoro scribes, skilled in the practice of divination and astrology with its attendant medicinal and magical implications, have travelled widely throughout the island.

The concept of destiny

The kind of cosmological system with which, into historic times, the practice of *katibo* from the south-east of the island so readily concurred may not have been of their own introduction. It is conceivable that a general acquaintance of the Malagasy people with Islamic systems of astrology rendered the specialised knowledge of the Antaimoro aristocracy especially pertinent. The principles from which this essentially predictive and practical view of the world derive are readily enough described as a set of overall propositions about the predetermined nature of human actions (the best account of the system is to be found in Ruud 1960). In offering some explanation of what is involved in Malagasy ideas it should be stressed that this is no rigid or inescapable calculation leading to unavoidable conclusions about individual fate; it is rather a system of interpretation. Furthermore, it is not fatalistic in character but offers the promise of a means of taking avoiding action, cheating what would otherwise be inevitable events and results.

The foundation of Malagasy ideas is the notion that everyone by virtue of the date and time of their birth inherits a particular destiny (*vintana*). *Vintana* might be described as an inexorable force that pervades and has the potential to dictate the world of human affairs. Particular months and days of the week possess good or bad *vintana*. The Malagasy terms for the lunar months and for the days of the week are both direct borrowings from the Arabic. Times of the day equally possess their own particular characteristics. Thus just before dawn is an especially auspicious time for a birth; a number of ceremonies, notably that of circumcision, are timed to coincide with sunrise; and the astrologer is renowned for finding his insight before the rising of the sun. (Indeed, one of the generic terms for a teller of the future is *mpanandro*, 'the maker or creator of the day'.) By contrast the middle of the night is a peculiarly inauspicious time to be born, and in fact in the past children born at that hour have been killed and the remains disposed of other than by incorporation into a family tomb, an act whose significance will become clear. At the very least a sacrificial offering will be required to sustain in life a child otherwise destined to be a potential witch.

Just as months, days and times of the day impose from birth a particular destiny, so as the individual moves through life he continually encounters zones of time with their associated potential for good or ill fortune. There are certain more or less established ground rules, although practice may vary. Broadly, each day is associated with particular colours, is more or less appropriate to particular kinds of work, and has its own taboos (*fady*) and prescribed sacrifice to remove or mollify any likely ill-effect. Thursday (Alakamisy), for example, is associated with the colour black. It is in general an awkward, troublesome day, a day associated with slaves. It is a reasonable day on which to hold a wedding but inadvisable for a funeral and thoroughly unreliable for performing divinations. A child born on a Thursday may have a black chicken swung over it to counteract any ill-effects from the opprobrium of the day. In planning a visit to Antaimoro country I was counselled against timing my arrival on a Thursday, the day of slaves; better to aim to arrive on a Friday (Zoma), a red day, the day of kings and of nobility. The implications of the advice in a society which, like the Antaimoro, holds to hierarchical ideas are self-evident: each day has its range of do's and dont's, its colours and associations.

Interpreting the interplay of personal *vintana* within these different arenas of astrological time is the work of the astrologer-diviner. He is able to explain the past and foretell the future. Clearly the matter becomes more complex when more than one person is involved, as, for instance, in a marriage or in establishing relations of blood brotherhood. The possibilities for further elaboration of the system are numerous and local variations in practice and degree of complexity extensive. For most people it is such ceremonial or ritual events which will require astrological advice, although in the past military campaigns, for example, might also be planned with the aid of an astrologer.

There is one further practical link between this more esoteric system of knowledge and common Malagasy practice. Astrology is not only about location in time; it is, in Madagascar, about locating time in space. Thus, the co-ordinates of the idea of *vintana* are expressed in a system of orientation so that it is not simply months, days or times of the day which have their different significance but also directions. The north/south axis is associated with the living. Houses are always, in principle, aligned north to south. The east/west axis is concerned with relations between the living and the dead, so doors are generally located to the west. Frequently this will be the sole method of entry and exit, although where a door does exist to the east it is rarely opened and then only on special occasions. When, for example, a corpse is laid out in a traditional hut, it will be aligned west to east with the head towards the open east door. The body itself may be taken out by this route emphasising the polarity of life and death which is expressed along this axis. Similarly, at circumcision boys may be operated upon facing east through an open door towards the rising sun. The opening of the east door in itself may imply the performance of some critical transitional rite in the life (and death) of the individual.

The plane conceived as lying between these cardinal points, that which runs north-east/south-west, is thus particularly important. The north-east is a sacred area associated with the dead and with the ancestors. Tombs are often sited to the north-east of settlements, and within a house the north-east corner is reserved for the storage of substances associated with the ancestors whether medicines, ritual objects, first fruits or even, in modern times, family documents. Other objects are equally stored according to the particular significance attached to the various quarters of a house which should ideally be a single-roomed single-floor rectangular dwelling. Different activities and most importantly seating at formal assemblies take account of the varying character of different orientations. Interestingly, where architectural form has diverged most from the idealised model of the single-roomed house, as, for instance, in the plateau, these rules elsewhere rigorously applied are reduced to what one author has called 'etiquette'. The first rule to be abandoned is strict alignment along a north/south axis.

Astrological time and space are not simply two parallel systems; they interrelate. The house, indeed, is at one level a model for thinking about *vintana*. Indeed, here is one compelling reason why there are no African round (and thus cornerless) huts found in Madagascar. The Malagasy conception of destiny with its roots in Islamic cosmology requires rectangles to make it 'thinkable'. This interrelatedness of *vintana* with space and spatial

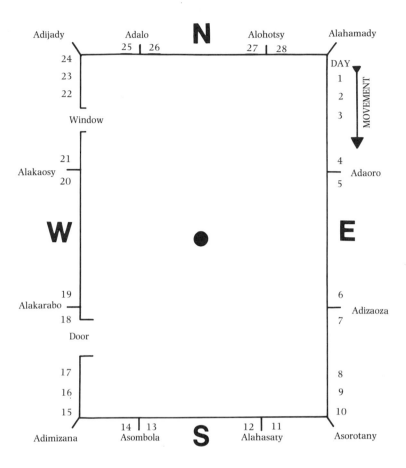

The *vintana* system.

organisation is evident in the practice of arranging the twelve lunar months around the house starting at the beginning of the year in the north-east corner with the first month of Alahamady in the Arabic calendar. The second month, Adaoro, lies towards the' east and so forth so that each month is allocated its place moving round the house in a clockwise direction. The circulating *vintana*, however, does not operate simply in one dimension of time. Thus the days of the month and by further elaboration the hours of the day might equally be conceived as circulating at their different paces.

Determining where *vintana* is located at any particular moment may be critical to deciding when to do certain things. The aim is always to avoid going against *vintana*. For instance, unless coming to a house directly from the west, a person is, in principle, obliged to take a clockwise course to the west-facing door. Clearly if the approach is made from the north, a circuit will need to be made to reach the westerly entrance (*A Glance at Madagascar* 1979, p. 61). However, it is on ritual occasions when this conjunction of *vintana* with the system of orientation is crucial and for this an astrologer will usually be needed, very often an Antaimoro or someone of Antaimoro background.

The rise of kingdoms

One other achievement sometimes credited to the Islamised populations who were settled in Madagascar by the middle of the present millennium is the creation of the circumstances in which hierarchical state organisations began to emerge. It has already been noted that Antaimoro clans may well have imposed their authority on some of their nearest neighbours. There is at least a viable model here from which to derive a situation in which small clan-based forms of social organisation might develop the kinds of interrelationships and interdependency which generate larger alliances of populations. The implications of a migrating people seeking to establish themselves in a new location is a possible mechanism.

The arrival of Europeans from the sixteenth century onwards is not merely incidental either. In August 1500 Diogo Dias commanding part of a Portuguese fleet seeking to open a route to India was blown off course and made landfall in Madagascar thus establishing the precise location of the large island already known to the Arab geographers. Various attempts at settlement followed in the succeeding centuries whether sponsored by European powers or necessitated by shipwreck. If these efforts now appear somewhat half-hearted, it is largely because the prize was not Madagascar itself but rather control of the spice trade with the East Indies. A foothold on the island was always useful; but conquest, in so far as it was even possible, was most unlikely to be worth the effort. It was not, in fact, until 1896 that the French ultimately took the island and established colonial rule. The attempt to create a base at Fort Dauphin in 1647 ultimately failed, as did all other efforts initially by the Portuguese and then by the Dutch and the British. Indeed, perhaps the most successful attempt at settlement was that undertaken by the ill-assorted bands of pirates and privateers who used the shelter of the Bay of Antongil, Île Sainte-Marie and eastern Madagascar as a major haven from which to attack shipping in the Indian Ocean and the Arabian Sea in the seventeenth and eighteenth centuries.

There is a habit of historical thinking which looks to major external events in explanation of apparently exceptional local ones. The African continent, whether it be the court of Benin in Nigeria or the kingdom centred on Great Zimbabwe with its formidable stone-walled enclosures, has been especially prone to speculation attributing indigenous developments to compelling outside influence. It is often as well to be circumspect in judging the effects of external events, real or assumed.

The Sakalava

In Madagascar the situation is rather unexpected. In historic times there have been three major movements towards state formations – those that resulted in the alliances of peoples whose heirs are today the Sakalava, the Betsimisaraka and the Merina. Of these the earliest and longest-lived is the development of state structures amongst the Sakalava, these evolving out of the establishment of the Maroserana dynasty amongst the Mahafaly in the south-west of the island. There has in recent years been some discussion of a possible African origin of this incipient ruling clan (Kent 1970, Brown 1978), but both local oral accounts and general historical opinion continue to accept an association with the Islamised groups of the south-east. In the century following the appearance of Europeans around the coast of Madagascar alliances between those communities already established in the south-west of the island and migrant peoples from the eastern seaboards led to the formation of the Volamena (literally, 'red silver' or 'gold') royal lineage. This by expansion and transplantation led in succeeding centuries to a northwards spread or unrolling of dynastic principles until by the nineteenth century the snowballing Sakalava kingdoms stretched the length of the west coast as far as Nosy Be in the north-west sector of the island. The relations between the various interrelated Sakalava dynasties and regions may not have been formalised and centralised in the manner of the more cohesive of state systems, but certainly the Sakalava retained an integrity which the Islamised peoples from whom they in part sprang did not. This integrity has been to an extent a question of shared cultural characteristics, of political, military and kin relationships.

'The many inseparables'

On the east coast the Betsimisaraka achieved their own form of unity albeit for a briefer period and less coherently than their name, 'the many inseparables', might imply. As a title the term Betsimisaraka was always as much a political slogan as a political fact. The peoples referred to occupy the long narrow coastal strip stretching from the Bay of Antongil as far south as Nosy Varika, some 650 km, and are today the second largest ethnic group on the island. It is a region dominated, particularly in the north, by dense tropical rain forest which contrives to isolate village communities – even those at a relatively short distance from the Indian Ocean coast. There remains as a result considerable cultural variation from one region to the next, differences in dialect, in ritual or local political office, in cultural practice, and in material culture. To a large extent traditional political organisation is still village-based and 'the many inseparables' a nostalgic tag.

The moment when it appeared that some broader military and political alliance might emerge occurred in the first decades of the eighteenth century. It centred on the person and achievements of one Ratsimilao, or Ramaromanompo ('the one who rules over many'), as he renamed himself to signal his success in uniting under his rule this extensive and disparate population. The crucial event which inspired this act of personal aggrandisement was his capture of the port of Fénérive in 1716 thereby defeating

Sakalava warrior carrying spear, shield, musket and powder horn and wearing protective charm necklace. From Sibree 1896, p. 149.

the Betanimena from the south who had formerly annexed to themselves ancestral lands belonging to the northerners including their tombs, some of which had been desecrated. Such annexation and destruction provided a powerful ideological focus around which Ratsimilao was able to assemble a cohesive force estimated to have reached at its peak upwards of some 10,000 strong. Further political and military activity contributed to the creation of a Betsimisaraka confederacy which endured until after 1750 and the death of Ratsimilao. In that time no lasting centralised institutions or other trappings and mechanisms of state administration were created and no royal lineage was effectively founded. Ratsimilao himself became more a prime minister than a king. The term in Malagasy appropriate to his standing is *filoha* which carries the sense of a charismatic leader and chief rather than that of a divine king. Ultimately the focus of cohesion provided by his person was not so readily inherited by his successors.

Who, then, was Ratsimilao? If in the background to the development of Sakalava kingdoms lies the influence of immigrant Islamised peoples, behind this brief flowering of Betsimisaraka unity rests the picturesque piratical tradition of Madagascar's east coast. By clan Ratsimilao was a Zanamalata, *malata* meaning 'mulatto' and referring to the children born of relations between a pirate father and a local Malagasy mother. At times well over 1,000 pirates might have resided in particular locations inter-marrying and interbreeding with the local population. Accounts written down in the 1760s identify Ratsimilao as the son of an English pirate known as Tamo (Tom) and the daughter of a chiefly family itself from Fénérive, the town he was to recapture. He was reputedly taken or sent to receive a Christian education in London while still young but returned after only a few months. Like many Zanamalata, Ratsimilao had access to the wealth, trade goods and fire-power which such paternity and control of trading relations established.

It is easy perhaps to overstress, or at least misunderstand, the benefits conferred by access to firearms, as the historian Berg has shown (1985). Both the Sakalava and Betsimisaraka essays in state development and con-federacy were in their different ways based in part on military activities. It would be tempting to link and explain these expansionist exercises, the one on the west coast, the other on the east, unequivocally to the encour-agement provided by imported musketry and gunpowder. Sakalava are very frequently portrayed and in later periods photographed carrying guns (see cover photograph). Still larger quantities of muskets probably reached the east coast where the slave trade was centred and developed from the seventeenth century. Indeed, Betsimisaraka, with some Sakalava participa-tion, used to seek slaves not only in the interiors of Madagascar itself but in the Comores and even along the African coast, using large modified canoes to mount sea-going expeditions. During the period from 1765 until 1820 as many as 500 such converted canoes might make an annual raid-ing party. Muskets were a significant item in the trade subsequently con-ducted with European slavers. Yet, as Berg points out, when it came to actual warfare at least on the east coast, traditional spears were often con-sidered altogether more reliable and effective weapons. Ratsimilao took

The harbour at the eastern coast port of Tamalave as it was in the 19th century with European trading ships in the bay. From Sibree 1870, p. 24.

Fénérive not by superiority of firearms – on that account he was massively outnumbered – as much as by superiority of tactics. Muskets, indeed, served ritual purposes rather than exclusively military ones and were often carried as ornaments rather than necessarily as intimidating weaponry. Finally the Betsimisaraka confederacy, despite the fact that it was already in some disarray, was unable to resist the expansionist aims of the Merina kingdom already developing by the turn of the century.

The Merina

This third emergent kingdom, and the last before French colonial occupation drew a veil over indigenous political developments of the kind, was in its inception at a remove from those external contacts which had sustained coastal populations. Indeed, in one of the most quoted remarks in Malagasy history, attributed to its most celebrated historical figure, Andrianampoinimerina, it was declared: 'the seas are the limits of my rice fields'. According to one possible reading of this statement, the ambition embedded in Merina expansion was not just that of a land-locked kingdom seeking access to the outside world merely to acquire exotic goods and technology. That no doubt was, or became, part of it; but the model at one level has affinity with that of some of the interior kingdoms of Africa where control over essentially local resources rather than privileged access to outside ones, or even necessarily the wish to obtain such access, provided the means and motive of political expansion.

By the late eighteenth century the Merina did not in fact need trade with Europeans to secure either the firearms on offer or for that matter many of the other items that formed part of economic interactions on the coast. Not only had they acquired significant stocks of musketry already through their own extensive trading networks, but Merina ironworkers were fashioning entirely viable local copies using recycled parts from European weapons. Furthermore, Imerina had little compelling need of imported cloth; it was, after all, an important weaving centre in its own right, producing in particular silk cloth which had for some time formed a part of its own export trade. Possession of a solid productive base, especially the ability to achieve high yields of rice, was perhaps one crucial element in the background to Merina expansion. Being distanced from the vagaries of external markets and international trade may account for the remarkable success of the Merina kingdom as readily as any presumed desire to participate in them.

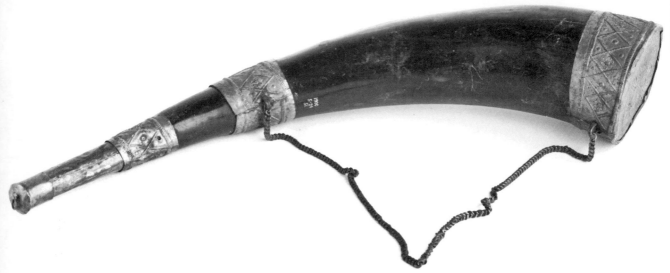

Powder horn with gold sleeving. Merina. L. 39 cm. BM 1900.5–24.51.

In the event, within a period of four decades from 1780 until 1820, the Merina, isolated in the high lands of the plateau and divided into innumerable small warring principalities, conquered much of the island, gained control of its ports, and established a monarchy that obliged European traders, missionaries or emissaries to trek into the interior to pursue their business rather than to conduct affairs solely at the coast. The foundations of this achievement were laid by Andrianampoinimerina.

In military terms what Andrianampoinimerina succeeded in doing is simply described. Declared king of the small fortified town of Ambohimanga and its surrounding acres in about 1780, he had within a period of fifteen or so years established himself and his capital at the nearby town of Antananarivo ousting after several attempts its ruler. A series of treaties and military campaigns enabled him to subdue the greater part of Imerina and remove any rivals to his authority over this once turbulent region. He expanded eastwards into Bezanozano country and south where by success in battle or by the imposition of vassal status the various Betsileo kingdoms were annexed to his own. The only area that remained relatively independent of its rapidly developing neighbour was that to the west where the Sakalava kingdoms successfully resisted Merina intrusion. Significantly, however, the kingdom which Andrianampoinimerina passed to his son Radama I at his death in 1810 already included all the most productive rice-producing areas of the island, in particular the vast terraced rice paddies of the Betsileo. To the east lay the forests of the Betsimisaraka with its diversified economy, to the west and south cattle-keeping country. Thus, although Radama did realise his father's ambition and extend the kingdom to the sea, he did not for all that greatly increase the area under rice cultivation.

Extending the rice fields to the sea, however, need not be taken as a literal statement; it is also a metaphor for the kingdom itself. The traditional unit of Merina society was and remains the *karazana* or *foko*, a unit that

Painting by Rainimaharosoa of the gateway to a fortified village in Imerina. Some of the large round stones were so heavy that it took up to forty men to roll them in and out of position.

has become known through the anthropological literature under the term 'deme' (after Bloch 1971, p. 46). This was in theory at least an endogamous group of people who were all related to each other by ties of blood. Geographically this basic social group occupied a defined territory comprising homesteads, rice fields and a common ancestral tomb. Over the centuries in the ebb and flow of political relationships individual rulers had emerged capable perhaps of uniting numbers of demes into small kingdoms. Initially Andrianampoinimerina was one of these. Having established his capital at Antananarivo, Ambohimanga in the demes from which he came was designated as the ritual centre of the kingdom. What distinguished

Opposite Rice being eaten off ravenala leaves with spoons made from the same leaves. The occasion is a ceremony at a remote forest site in Betsimisaraka country. At such events the process of cooking is carried out by men who also serve it to women reversing the usual domestic situation.

Silver coinage as used in Madagascar, particularly in Imerina. The number of coins acquired in trade with the outside world was inadequate for local needs. Coins were therefore cut in order to extend the quantities in circulation and their value in part was assessed by weight. Uncut coins were offered in return for expected ancestral blessings. Max. diam. 1.5 cm. BM 1900.5–24.5.

Andrianampoinimerina from others who had similarly come to preside over an expanding 'demedom', however, was in part the skill he possessed in creating and maintaining the administration of this innovative political system. The demes were each arranged within a hierarchical structure: some naturally profited, not least those of Avaradrano with Ambohimanga at their centre. This much was routine; the skill, however, lay in manipulating the structure to create appropriate niches for potential rivals and power blocks within the system. Beyond that he was able to exploit the demes as communes that might undertake vaster projects lying beyond their own more limited ancestral territories. From this successful extension of traditional modes of social action derives the massive increase in rice production which is traditionally credited to his personal innovations.

This was not simply a matter of acquiring additional rice fields by conquest and annexation; in the first place large-scale public works were initiated which transformed the marshes and plains, especially those round

Gold jewelled crown said to have been the reserve of the royal clan. Merina, 19th century.
Diam. 19 cm. 1900.5–24.1.

Ornament of gold with silk brocaded sash; the form is here suggestive of a talisman. Such
ornaments were worn round the waist as illustrated (*opposite*) in the portrait of Rafaralahy,
a Merina military governor.
Merina, said to date from AD 1820 or shortly after.
L. 19 cm. 1900.5–24.34.

Opposite Portrait of Rafaralahy, Merina governor of Foule Point, a coastal fort
on the island's east coast. From Ellis 1838.

Rice being prepared for a ceremony. Here it is being pounded and winnowed by Betsimisaraka women. Rice is an inevitable part of the feasting which takes place on such occasions.

the capital itself, into productive land suitable for traditional wet-rice cultivation. Equally important, however, the engineering involved in making dikes, irrigation canals and drainage systems on a large scale permitted for the first time the growth of a second significant crop within a single year. This is known as *vary aloha* ('first rice'), a reference to the fact that it is sown in the dry season and brought on by irrigation rather than planted out only when the rains are assured. The work that made this possible was directed by the sovereign, as was the distribution of the produce. The royal astrologers made the calculations necessary to establish the most propitious time cosmologically and climatically for the various agricultural operations involved. *Vary aloha* was also the rice used in first fruit ceremonies and that traditionally offered to the royal family. 'Rice and I', Andrianampoinimerina declared, 'are one'. Although this paraphrases a larger statement, it recalls both that the sovereign held significant rights over proportions of the harvest and that inventions and innovations credited to him transformed the physical and economic landscape of Imerina. Finally, rice was also in some senses a sacred substance – and in that respect partook of characteristics that increasingly came to be attributed to the person of the sovereign himself.

The divinity of kings

When comparing the three political systems to have emerged within historic times, it would seem that that of the Betsimisaraka was the only one that did not elevate its ruler to the status of a unifying ritual figure with overtly religious characteristics. No doubt this is related to the temporary and ephemeral nature of the Betsimisaraka confederacy. Elsewhere the sanctity of the royal person was most clearly displayed in those ceremonies which he performed on behalf of his subjects or those which endorsed his mystical authority. For instance, the ritual of the royal bath (*fandroana*) in its various forms survived to be recorded and documented in some detail for the Merina and the Sakalava, and also the Antaimoro (Sibree 1900, Abinal 1949–50, Molet 1956 and 1979). This event took place annually, timed to coincide with the birth of the new moon in the lunar month of Alahamady, the beginning of the year and the month associated with things sacred, with the north-east, the ancestors – and with the king. In Imerina it was also tied in to the agricultural year and especially the cycle of activity in the rice fields occasioned as the dry season gives way to the rains.

Meat divided up and laid out subsequent to a sacrifice so that participants may each take an equal share. A number of procedures may be followed on such occasions: frequently specified portions may be smoked in honour of the ancestors, while other parts are boiled and cooked separately for the consumption of the majority of those present. Bezanozano.

The central act of the royal bath, most elaborately described by nineteenth-century missionaries to Imerina, was the moment when the sovereign removed old used clothing and entered the bath of warmed water. The water was collected from certain streams and lakes with sacred associations and mixed with earth collected from the royal tombs. Not only those of royalty but all tombs were left open during the ceremony. As the sovereign emerged, head and hair damp, and arrayed in new finery, some of the water from the bath was dispersed on the subjects present in an act of royal blessing. This was the signal for the same ritual to be performed by senior members of households throughout the kingdom. The dispersal

Necklace of uncut silver coins as offered in soliciting blessing. Merina. L. 74 cm. BM +4684.

of the water is linked to the granting of *hasina*, a mystical quality regarded as capable of rendering something viable and efficacious. The authority to dispense *hasina* was an attribute supremely invested in the sovereign. He or she controlled its dispersal both directly – in this instance through the sprinkling of water – and indirectly in determining the timing of similar events everywhere else in Imerina.

In terms of materials the Merina royal bath was reputedly of silver, like royal coffins. Silver came from melted-down coinage, uncut coins being traditionally offered as a means of soliciting *hasina*. More generally, however, the association of the bath and the coffin introduces another level of interpretation of the ritual. It is tempting to link the cleansing and rewrapping of the sovereign with the process of periodically removing the bones of the deceased from the ancestral tomb and reclothing them in a fresh shroud. Such a process of purification and renewal is practised throughout Imerina. Significantly, only royalty were left in the first place of burial and neither retombed nor subsequently rewrapped. The annual bathing of the live sovereign, it could be argued, performed the act of cleansing on behalf of the royal dead, and the act of renewal on behalf of the kingdom. This was only possible because the sovereign was regarded as

Silver charm in the form of a zebu said to be made to attract wealth and as such recorded in a number of parts of the plateau region. The long horns on this image recall the herds of royal cattle, the preserve of high-ranking Merina. L. 6 cm. BM 1900.5–24.9.

already possessed of mystical qualities otherwise associated with the ancestors.

The equivalent ceremony amongst the Sakalava (who do not practise second burial either for kings or commoners) is the washing of the royal relics and royal regalia. This takes place at the beginning of the first lunar month, and the relics are either taken and washed in an estuary or otherwise refurbished with a purifying concoction made from honey and water. The association with processes of death and regeneration are also emphasised here, as are the regenerative powers of royalty.

In a similar vein royalty had access to all the best magic in the kingdom. They were advised by *ombiasy*, the class of astrologers, diviners and healers, and also controlled the use of charms. There are two kinds of charm familiar in Madagascar: the commonest are *ody*, personal talismans that might ensure good fortune or, in the nineteenth century, act as a protection in battle. Formulas written in *Sorabe* script might be used in this manner, as they were on behalf of the Antanosy as a group when the French attempted to establish a base in the south-east of the island. Other prominent examples are the carved images, worn by the Bara, which amongst others included small representations of coffins said to attract the spirit of an enemy who might then be trapped. The Merina for their part carried both wooden figurative images (which like the Sakalava royal relics were treated periodically with honey) and also crocodile teeth. The crocodile is virtually the only formidible carnivore found in Madagascar; it is hardly surprising, therefore, that it should be employed when the island's ethnozoology is so short on prominent creatures through which to express relations of power. Ornaments including representations of crocodile teeth in silver and gold were also worn as insignia by high-ranking Merina.

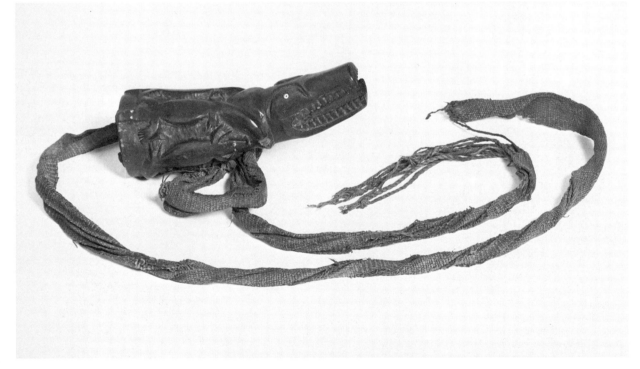

Wood war charm in the form of a crocodile, a powerful image for the Malagasy and containing protective magical substances. Said to be Sakalava. L. 14 cm. BM +1618.

Perhaps the commonest *ody* were slivers of wood which might stand on their own as a protector or be incorporated into other images. Of all these the most powerful were those derived from a class of exceptional talismans known as *sampy* which were operated by priests at the behest of the Merina ruler. These were ranked according to their powers and had attributed to them the ability to protect the army, ensure victory and conquest, reveal the appropriate times for action, and otherwise safeguard the interests of the kingdom. Andrianampoinimerina, for instance, sought for a year to gain support of the most renowned *sampy* in Imerina, the talisman called Rakelimalaza. In the end he gained access to its powers only by promoting the people who were its hereditary guardians to noble status. Gain-ing control of the *sampy* was every bit as important as winning the allegiance of the deme in whose control it resided.

One of the fuller accounts of what these royal *sampy* actually looked like describes Ramahavaly, one of the most celebrated, being ranked only just beneath Rakelimalaza:

> And in the other box was the idol itself, which they called Ingahibe. (Perhaps the nearest, and not inappropriate, translation of this word is 'The Old Gentleman'.) This consisted of two pieces of wood, seven finger-breadths in length, and about the size of one's wrist in thickness. And their coverings were: first, dark blue cloth; secondly, native silk cloth; and thirdly, scarlet cloth; and they were also annointed with castor-oil and with a gum used for burning incense; and between them were coral beads and pieces of silver and white beads; and outside they were ornamented with pieces of scarlet cloth and dark blue cloth, so that the appearance was like a bird having wings and head, the body glittering with the different beads fastened to it . . .

This account was written down by Rainivelo who saw Ramahavaly on 9 September 1869 (it was published translated from an original manuscript in Rainivelo 1875, p. 113). He was, however, the last to see the celebrated talisman for, as a Christian convert and pastor, he had been sent to burn it in the name of Queen Ranavalona II. The other *sampy* were similarly destroyed, including Rakelimalaza which turned out to be a small piece of wood wrapped in scarlet cloth and with silver chains attached. This act of destruction, ordered in direct opposition to the devotees and guardians of the royal talismans by a Merina sovereign baptised in the Christian faith, marked a turning-point in the island's history. A central focus of state unity and order was abolished; with it, however, also went a major support to the system of noble status. What followed was inevitable – a period of adjustment and realignment as a wholly new set of circumstances emerged.

Left A personal talisman (*ody*) from the southern part of Imerina. The upper part of the figure detaches to reveal a cavity within which magical substances are kept. The figure was rescued from destruction in the 19th century and is one of a male and female pair. Private collection. H. 20 cm.

Right Drawing of a *sampy*, sent to England in 1833 to encourage support for missionary activity which was aimed at the eradication of such idols. This example subsequently disappeared. From Ellis 1838, vol. 2, p. 477.

The European legacy

Traditional musical forms remain unimpaired by outside influences; the instruments used, however, have changed. In the east the accordion is common, while elsewhere local versions of guitars and, as here, violins are made. Betsimisaraka.

T he first mission school was opened in Madagascar as early as 1818 at Tamatave on the east coast; it had very few pupils and was short-lived. Indeed, from the two Welsh mission families who established it only one person, David Jones, survived, the others falling victim to what was presumably virulent malaria in the space of six months. Two years later, however, Jones had returned and established a mission school in Imerina itself with the consent of Andrianampoinimerina's successor, Radama I. Initially his pupils were all children of the royal household and teaching

was in English. Within a short time Jones and a second missionary sent by the Nonconformist London Missionary Society (LMS), David Griffiths, gained a command of Malagasy so that by 1824 they were well able to preach in the native language. The use of a Roman rather than Arabic alphabet and script was agreed upon enabling a translation of the New Testament to be virtually completed only five years after Jones's arrival in Imerina. The Bible itself was ready in printed translation by 1835, and the first English-Malagasy dictionary had been prepared. Artisans were also brought in during the 1820s making available the skills of European blacksmithing, of carpenters, spinners and printers.

Christianity itself, in its institutional setting, was by no means antithetical to traditional Merina practice. The deme provided a ready basis for congregational gatherings; the sermon – no matter how lengthy – cohered well with the Malagasy tradition of colourful and inventive oratory. The Christian faith, however, was clearly at odds with many areas of traditional belief and especially that in the efficacy of *ody* and *sampy*. There was, therefore, throughout the nineteenth century a continuous flux and tension between the adherents of traditional ideas and the innovative European culture which became accessible in the first instance through missionary activity.

This flux is evident in the attitudes of monarchs no less than in those of their subjects. The encouragement to missionary teaching provided by Radama I contrasted sharply with the stance taken by his successor, Queen Ranavalona I, who in 1835 banished missionaries from the kingdom and periodically throughout her reign persecuted practising Malagasy Christians. Some 200 were martyred and others forced into exile or reduced from positions of influence to slavery. Yet paradoxically, although the Queen banned printed books, the development of a literate class under missionary influence was important to her in enabling the development of state institutions, strengthening and codifying the affairs of the kingdom. Paradoxically too it could be argued that in expelling the missionaries, and in making martyrs of some of her own subjects, she created the very circumstances that ensured the survival of the Christian elements in Merina society. Indeed, the indigenous roots thus cultivated for this exotic faith permitted it to flourish once her reign was at an end. Madagascar was to become in the latter part of the nineteenth century one of the most successful fields of Christian missionary endeavour.

Radama II readmitted the missionary societies in 1861 and, although he himself was assassinated by the traditionalists, Ranavalona II and subsequently Ranavalona III maintained close associations with the missionaries making Christianity something of a royal cult. From as early as 1862 Protestantism became the official state religion, a somewhat curious development given that the Nonconformity of the LMS, which more than any other Society was responsible for the initiatives which led to these developments, was fashioned in opposition to ideas of national religions. Elsewhere on the island Catholic, Episcopalian, Quaker and various Evangelical missions each had their own allocated area in which to preach their faith.

Radama II and his wife, subsequently herself proclaimed Queen under the name Rasoherina. From Ellis 1859, p. 412.

European influences

The effects wrought by the sustained presence of a growing European community – expanded to include traders and soldiers brought in to train the Merina army – were many and complex. It would be excessive to identify all changes with missionary activity, especially in the field of the arts. Certainly church-going was extensive. By the time of French colonisation in 1895 the LMS alone could claim some quarter of a million adherents, the total throughout the island being perhaps twice that number (although not all necessarily communicant). Ecclesiastical buildings were erected, amongst the first being stone-built churches dedicated to the memory of the Malagasy martyrs and erected at the sites where they met their deaths. In Imerina and southwards into Betsileo country brick-making allowed for the gradual replacement of the traditional one-roomed, one-storeyed wooden structures, seen in the nineteenth-century illustrations, by the more elaborate dwellings of today. Only in the remoter forested area occupied by the Zafimaniry does the original form of wood-planked housing survive. Amongst the first essays in refabrication was the brick-cladding added to the impressive wooden palace (*rova*) originally built for Queen Ranavalona I by the Frenchman Jean-Baptiste Laborde. Although a 'secular' building (in so far as its occupation by the Merina sovereign allows of such description), the brickwork was in fact added by James Cameron, a Scotsman, and significantly one of the original mission-artisans recruited for work in Madagascar by the LMS. Inside houses and the palace alike European styles of furniture were increasingly found, amongst the more popular being wooden beds, many incorporating designs and motifs in the Empire style.

Fashions in dress too began to change, especially amongst higher-placed Merina. The tradition of trading as an appropriate activity for people of standing, whatever else they may also engage in, was well-established – Andrianampoinimerina himself was reputedly a wealthy and successful

The area of Antananarivo dominated by the imposing structure of the royal palace, here rendered in wood, as it was in the mid-19th century. In addition to the royal dwellings the traditional wooden housing of Imerina is seen on the slopes of the town. From Oliver 1866, p. 67.

High-ranking Merina attired in the
European styles already available in
central Madagascar by the mid-19th
century. From Oliver 1866, p. 64.

Ranavalona III photographed in exile
in Algiers where she was banished
subsequent to French colonial takeover
and where she died in 1917. Her
remains were returned amidst great
ceremony for burial in Antananarivo
in 1938.

trader. Trade came increasingly to include European garments. The
monarchy dressed as European monarchy so that Ranavalona III appeared
in public in the crown and robes of royalty, and her own personal jewellery
included pieces made by the leading French jewellery houses of the late
nineteenth century. It was Radama I, however, who started the practice
of drawing on European models, and his portrait shows him in appropriate
dress. He was also an admirer of the exploits of Napoleon as retold to him
by Europeans, and the murals in Palais D'Argent, indeed, include a
silhouette of Napoleon. The army, too, began to be equipped in uniforms
derived from European military dress of the period.

A more directly mission-inspired initiative was the teaching in all its pro-
fusion of techniques of lace-making at which Malagasy women became
extremely proficient. The credit for this innovation lies with Mrs Selina Wills
who began teaching it from 1882 at Ambohimanga where her husband
was LMS missionary. Subsequently it was taken up at Fianarantsoa providing additional income and a further diversification of female craftwork
(J. T. Hardyman, personal communication).

Such mission-led teaching was undoubtedly responsible for many similar
developments elsewhere, some taken further during the French colonial
period with the creation of Ecoles and Ateliers d'Art Appliqué beginning
in 1896 at Antananarivo. Additional centres were created at Tulear,
Ampanihy and elsewhere in the present century. That established at
Ambositra drew on a tradition already initiated in the nineteenth century
by resident missionaries. Amongst the early specialities was work in horn
and a number of missionary collections formed in the area include such
items as cups, bottles and spoons rendered in horn stained various colours.
The first two objects were possibly developed out of communion cups and
bottles. Later Ambositra became famous as a centre of marquetry and in
the last few decades has evolved other lines in furniture and figurative carving. This work is especially associated with the Zafimaniry and, indeed,
many objects are still blocked out and prepared in the forest villages of

nearby Zafimaniry country, particular communities having their speciality, only being brought to Ambositra for finishing and ultimately to be marketed. In its modern developments much of this has taken place under the influence and direction of the French Catholic missions in the area.

Writing and design

However, the most significant of those missionary legacies that are not directly religious in character is unquestionably literacy. Literacy rates in Madagascar are remarkably high and particularly in Imerina where writing was first taught. A significant literature has grown up both in Malagasy and by Malagasy writing in French. Indeed, it is little known that the words to such popular songs as 'Ain't Misbehavin' (with Thomas 'Fats' Waller in 1929) and 'Memories of You' (with Eubie Blake in 1930) were the work of one Andy Razaf, a Merina but of American birth (J. Picton, personal communication). 'Andy' would seem to be a shortening of Andriana ('noble').

Woman's raffia skirt (*sadia*) with an invocation woven along its border. This imitates the proverbs, vows and statements found on the printed commercial cloth women use as wrap-around skirts. The process of *weaving* words using, as here, the traditional loom is technically very difficult. The invocation translates as 'Bless me in my work, O God, that I may prosper'. Betsimisaraka. W. 74 cm. BM 1984.Af14.152.

Writing, however, has not simply enabled the development of a tradition of Malagasy literature; it also has implications for the history of vernacular design in Madagascar. Firstly written formulas of various kinds – statements of good intent, of welcome, and often proverbs – appear on many types of object. These range from mats hung on walls to hats and baskets

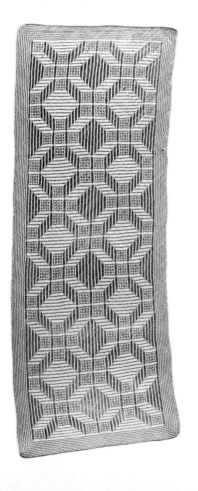

MISAORA AN'IJEHOVAH
RY FANAHIKO

Mat with a text offering thanks to God, as hung on an Antaimoro wall. W. 137 cm. MAA 76–1–33.

Mat showing the elaboration of design typical of much Malagasy basketry and mat-making. Antandroy. W. 160 cm. BM 1985.Af17.225.

which have words woven into the actual structure of the object. Printed *lamba* ('cloth') which is available throughout the island, as indeed on the Swahili coast of East Africa, will have an epithet included in its design. There are regional variations and preferences according to the nature of the statement. Even woven cloth may include sentences, this being an exceptionally difficult technical feat using only the simple single-heddle loom. Mats with inscriptions of the 'Bless this house' variety may well have been the initial inspiration of this tradition and would seem again to be associated with mission influence.

Design and pattern are themselves often described in Malagasy by reference to writing whether or not they include actual inscription. A basketry hat can be 'a hat with writing' even if it has only geometric design and no words. A hierarchy which runs from letter to word and sentence is often invoked in discussion to describe aspects of pattern, whether an individual element, the complete motif, or the overall conception of the design. This is so whether or not the person speaking is necessarily literate, and indeed the objects on which written inscription does appear may even be executed by someone who is unable to write and must simply copy the formula from elsewhere. It is also interesting that all the objects to which these observations apply – plaited basketwork of a variety of sorts and woven textiles – are produced by women or, in the case of the printed *lamba*, generally worn by women.

What all this suggests is a link between writing and the development of intricate systems of design. Certainly today every major centre in Madagascar has its range of basketry and mats which are frequently produced in villages in the remoter hinterland. Each centre has its identifiable styles with variations in pattern and degree of elaboration. It can be argued that the enthusiasm with which writing was taken up in Madagascar was not just a question of the broader acceptance of European culture but can be related specifically to the older tradition of writing as practised exclusively by the exponents of *Sorabe*. (Compare, for instance, Bloch 1968.) It was making available wisdom formerly accessible only to Islamised scribes. For the non-literate design and pattern merge into writing, and written formulas of the kind displayed on many objects have an esoteric and not merely a literal aspect.

59

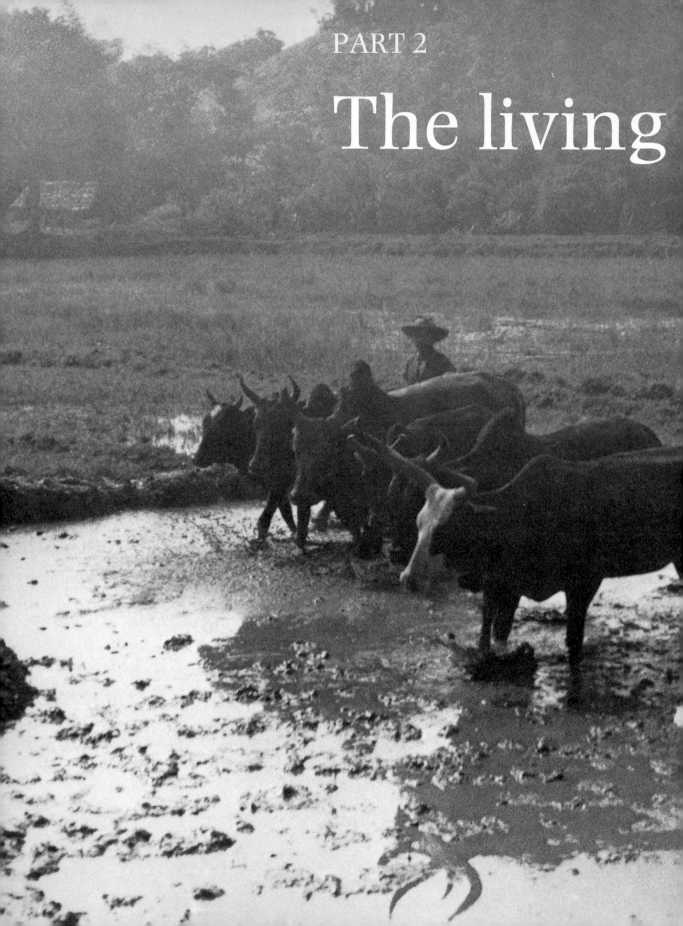

PART 2

The living

and the dead

The concept of 'the ancestors'

Invocation to the ancestors made over the sacrificial beast. The sacred east-facing passage is kept clear except for bottles of alcohol and soft drinks subsequently offered to the participants. Officials and audience alike have a white dot on the forehead made with a substance which is otherwise taken by mediums to induce spirit possession. Betsimisaraka.

Pages 60–1 Preparing paddy-fields before planting out rice. Along the wet eastern coastline conventional ploughing is impossible; here cattle, otherwise kept largely for sacrificial purposes, are also chased round paddies to churn up the mud.

The Malagasy have an enviable reputation for the extent of their knowledge of the medicinal properties of the island's unique flora. Some of the species used medicinally – the periwinkle, for instance – have long been known and exploited elsewhere as well. Yet in Madagascar all the larger markets have a corner set aside at which traders dispense hundreds of different types of roots, leaves, seeds or charms gathered together from all parts of the island, and each with a recognised medical function. Even if untested scientifically, they are implicitly accepted as efficacious by many Malagasy. It is not simply a question of falling back on a traditional remedy where modern medicines might otherwise be difficult to obtain; in many cases, and particularly where the condition is more urgent and potentially serious, like a scorpion sting, the locally available antidote is preferred.

Especially in the countryside and in more remote areas traditional healers (*ombiasy*) have a considerable following. Their range of remedies may be more restricted than those available in urban centres, and their alternatives fewer, but their prestige can be enormous. By contrast with the urban stall holder they are not simply dispensing herbal or magical remedies anonymously as a conventional chemist might and relying on the medicinal qualities of the substance to effect a cure. Indeed, subsequent to consulting an *ombiasy* the prognosis may not be the need to take or apply a medicine at all; it might, for instance, be instruction to perform a sacrifice or other cultural action. *Ombiasy* are heirs to a tradition of esoteric lore and practice according to which illness or other misfortune may have more than a purely physical cause. Remedial action may therefore involve more than purely physical application; it can equally include other activities often involving reference to the ancestors (*razana*).

Amongst the Betsimisaraka the *ombiasy* is not just concerned with present maladies; he is also a diviner, as skilled at foretelling the future as at seeking out the cause of any current malaise. He can fashion charms and amulets (*ody*), whose manipulation might equally serve therapeutic ends. Others elsewhere are reputed to have made charms that had the power to stop bullets. Treatment might additionally include strictures to observe individual or collective taboos (*fady*) often dealing with dietary questions. The span of advice and ministration offered extends to preventive as well as more directly curative measures. In no case, however, is medicine (*fanafody*) likely to be prescribed in isolation from other measures, and cer-

Bara *ombiasy* with magical and medicinal devices strung from his neck. He also wears a necklace of different wood and mineral substances, slivers from which might be used in making up medicinal compounds. From Marcuse 1914, p. 101.

An orator making his pocket accessible to receive coins, a mark of recognition by his audience of a point well made and a means of associating with the more general ancestral blessing sought in the sacrifice of a zebu which follows. Betsimisaraka.

tainly never without an appropriate invocation. Its efficacy is associated with these additional features of the treatment, and the sale of medicines in a market independently of actions and words performed by an *ombiasy* is already at a remove from traditional practice.

To collect medicines for museological purposes is clearly an exceptional circumstance, and the procedures to be followed have to an extent to be invented to fit this rather special case. The medicines themselves were mostly of wood, lengths cut from smaller branches, some leaves and seeds, the last used not so much as a medicine as in divination. There were also a number of manufactured objects including a spent cartridge case in green plastic. Each had a particular medical purpose, one species of wood as an antidote to constipation, the cartridge case as a cure for infertility in women. After discussion the process decided upon was to bring a bowl of water mixed with local rum (*toakagasy*) into which coins of small denomination were thrown by those present. The *ombiasy* then made a lengthy invocation to the ancestors; a sliver cut from each of the medicines was in turn mixed up in the bowl, the addition of each successive compound being the occasion for further invocation; and a sample was at the same time set aside. Finally the infusion of all the various compounds, the water and the rum was drunk by those present and authority granted to acquire the samples.

The form of this small ceremony is drawn from aspects of that which might take place in an actual consultation on a medical question. The most significant feature, however, is the invocation. In each case it was preceded by a high-pitched whistling sound emitted by the *ombiasy* which is characteristic of addresses to the ancestors. The tossing of coins into the water is equally an act which, as its occurrence in other contexts makes clear, is intended to entice ancestral presence and specifically ancestral blessing. At sacrifice, for instance, it is customary amongst the Betsimisaraka for humorous speeches to be made in advance of the more formal invocation uttered over the sacrificial animal. As observations are made which the audience judge apposite or witty, people rush forward from the crowd to fill the speaker's pockets with money. The procedure is more than simply a means of rewarding an impressive or entertaining performance; it is at the same time a token of the co-operative presence of the ancestors which is sought at the more solemn events that are to follow. Elsewhere, amongst the Sakalava, for instance, royalty are buried with coins in their mouths, the coins being a precondition of royal spirits speaking out which they do through spirit mediums (Feeley-Harnik, forthcoming).

In consultation the money (*vola*) is associated with the invocation made by the *ombiasy* (*joro*, 'an invocation', or more generally, as Feeley-Harnik points out, *vola/na*, 'speech'); but the money is tossed into the bowl. The invocation, in other words involves speech, but it is also intended to make the medicines mixed up in the bowl 'speak'. An invocation might mention individual ancestors by name or might simply invoke the ancestors as a community. Either way associating with the power of ancestors to bless, heal and cure is seen as essential to the effectiveness of a medical treatment. The money helps to localise these effects in the compound being prepared.

Opposite (top) Elaborately patterned cloth of a kind woven originally as an exercise in skill for sale to Europeans. Despite the complexity of its design, it has been woven on the traditional single-heddle loom. Such cloth was subsequently acquired by Malagasy themselves amongst whom it was used as a particularly impressive burial shroud (*lamba mena*). Merina. W. 177 cm. BM 1949.Af10.1; J. Keeves Esq.

Opposite (bottom) Ornaments of silver with bead sheaths. The form recalls that of a personal talisman (*ody*) both in the use of beads and the representation of crocodile teeth which were carried by Merina soldiers as amulets. Here these various references have been assembled in an emblem of high military office. Merina, said to date from 1800. L. 8 cm. BM 1900.5–24.33.

Knife with brass handle and iron blade, used either in circumcision or sacrifice. The scene shows a circumcision. On the underside of the knife in relief is a crocodile. Sakalava. L. 33 cm. MAA 61–10–103.

To make the medicine speak is to make it efficacious, much as a person possessed by a spirit (*tromba*) will be ill until the spirit is induced to speak. This it does when enticed and cajoled out of the body of the possessed so that the person may shake and tremble and speak inarticulately. These words reinterpreted by a spirit medium provide the reasons why someone has been thus afflicted and indicate appropriate effective remedial actions.

Ancestors are by no means the only spiritual entities recognised in Malagasy cosmology. God in the Christian sense is equated with Andriamanitra ('the fragrant lord'), Andrianahary ('the creator') or in some regions Zanahary. The ancestors rank with the Vazimba, the original occupiers of the land, certain legendary beings and other secondary divinities; but the concept of the ancestors is a much more pervasive point of reference. Collecting medicines is one thing for their very efficacy as medicines draws on ancestral intervention. Even to discuss questions of tradition and history, things 'of the ancestors', with village elders in any relatively formal setting may well involve some form of invocation or ceremony, however truncated. At the very least a communal sharing of *toakagasy* is likely to be indispensable, a quantity being poured in the north-east corner of the hut in honour of the ancestors. In the case of the Merina their oral tradition is to some extent recorded and accessible in the *Tantaran'ny Andriana* (Callet 1873), a large document of unparalleled value as a source for historians and anthropologists alike. This, however, is exceptional. Elsewhere access to local historical traditions, as to other forms of ancestral knowledge, even down to relatively mundane questions of traditional practice, must normally involve seeking appropriate ancestral authority.

The concept of the ancestors is thus a crucial one in Malagasy life. Indeed, ultimately the idea of the ancestors (*razana*) encompasses and expresses all that is considered morally desirable or appropriate in social relations. That notions of good conduct have the authority of ancestral precedent can already be detected in the fact that the final sanction for grosser violations of acceptable behaviour is exclusion from the ancestral tomb. At death the body of a malefactor will be disposed of otherwise than by incorporation with the remains of their kin, an act which disbars them from entrance

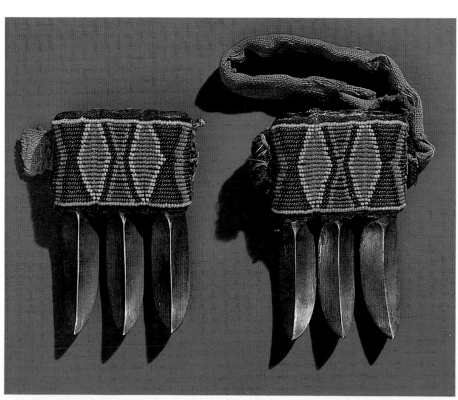

into the community of the ancestors, effectively equivalent to being condemned to eternal oblivion. At the same time this ensures that the moral authority of the concept of *razana* remains unsullied and intact. If the historical processes by which Malagasy culture has been assembled are various, constant reference to the ancestors is none the less a basic and pervasive theme.

This is hardly unusual. The overdrawn implications of the term 'ancestor worship' which affixed itself to the description of many traditional societies have been hard to shake off, at least in the more popular literature. Locating oneself in terms of membership of a kin group, imbuing the dead with the qualities of spirits, and seeing good and bad fortune in terms of their influence on the world of the living are common enough cultural features. What makes Malagasy practice distinctive is the degree to which this concept structures so many areas of everyday experience, for example, the twin supports of the traditional Malagasy economy, rice and cattle. Neither is simply a source of nourishment.

Reference to rice (*vary*) is the basis of many sayings and proverbs; it is also an important standard of measurement. The weight of quantities of rice was a significant measure. Rice also provided models for measuring time and even by extension distance. The agricultural calendar was constructed in terms of the cycle of rice growth, and the first planting and other significant moments in the production of the crop remain important ritual occasions. Distance might in its turn be measured by reference to the cooking of rice. Thus the distance between two points might be expressed in terms of the time it would take to travel between them, this calculated as the number of pots of rice that could be prepared in the interval. Moreover, just as the Inuit (or Eskimo) have a large vocabulary for the description of snow, so the Malagasy, amongst the largest *per capita* consumers of rice in the world, have an elaborate range of terms by which to describe the condition of rice.

As well as constituting something of a cultural obsession, rice is considered holy (*masina*); it is the food appropriate to human beings, eaten at every meal, even on its own, and an inescapable element in the feasting that accompanies ritual events. Rice is the product of paddy-fields which, being inherited within single families or clans, represent the toil of now-deceased generations of kinsmen. Tombs may also be located within the same areas of ancestral land. To this extent rice expresses a link between the living, their ancestors and a particular place, and all manner of cultural practice flows therefrom. There are, for instance, differences of opinion in Madagascar as to whether a little rice should be left at the end of a meal in honour of the ancestors or not. In some places it is; elsewhere it is held to entail the risk of being dispersed in inappropriate ways. The subject is not a neutral one; rice is not just food, it is equated with life and with vitality (Bloch 1985, pp. 634–5), and as such inextricably bound up with ideas concerning ancestral action.

Many of the island's main cattle-keeping regions are also rice-producing, even if yields and the area of land under cultivation are small by comparison with the intensively terraced paddy-fields of central Madagascar. Indeed,

Wood spoon of a kind developed out of a less elaborate ladle for preparing and serving rice. Possibly Sakalava. L. 31 cm. BM 1947.Af18.103.

Opposite Antaimoro scholar-astrologer (*katibo*) reading from the *Sorabe* ('great writings'). His clothing, like the book itself, evokes the Islamic element in Malagasy culture.

Basketry hat surmounted by the image of the humped zebu. In the south herdsmen also wear hats made from the tail hair of cattle and the skin of the hump itself. Leather is used for making objects as diverse as sandals and slings. Antandroy. H. 15 cm.
BM 1985.Af17.101.

manioc and sweet potato are also produced as a supplement to rice, especially in the south where they may even be said to replace it. Cattle are used for tilling the fields, but they are very much more than simply working animals. A more appropriate model is that of cattle-keeping in Eastern Africa where the herd is at once an expression of wealth, a subject of intense aesthetic interest, and possesses a religious significance that extends any more direct economic or utilitarian function the beasts may perform.

As with rice, an association of cattle with the ancestors is clearly present in Malagasy ideas. In this way the continuity of the herd and of the clan are related. Firstly, cattle are marked to indicate ownership, their ears being cut and indented according to a formula or pattern appropriate to each group of kinsmen. This clan 'blueprint' is termed *sofindrazana* ('the ancestral ear'). In addition their horns are trained (as amongst Nilotic peoples in Africa) so that as they grow they form arcs and curves, each of which has its particular term in Malagasy. An elaborate vocabulary is also available for the description of the pattern and the combination of colours of individual animals, and particular colours and horn shapes are regarded as fortuitous. This can be significant in selecting an animal for sacrifice, a ceremony which, except sometimes at funerals, always involves a formal address to the ancestors performed over the animal immediately prior to the act of sacrifice itself. Such sacrifice often has as its overt purpose the seeking of ancestral blessing or the rendering of thanks for ancestral favour. Cattle are thus converted from mere beasts into a channel of communication with the ancestors.

66

Burial, reburial and famadihana

I nevitably the process of burial, the act of effecting the cultural transitions from being merely human to becoming an ancestor, is an important focus of Malagasy ideas. Similarly, that complex of artefacts which includes tombs, shrouds, coffins and memorials of various kinds is the outstanding feature of the island's material culture. Several aspects of this treatment of the dead have already been mentioned. The process of burial is not necessarily a single event for the Malagasy; in some cases the remains of deceased kinsmen are returned to on repeated occasions with the result that burial or funerary practice merges into a more general relationship to the ancestors. Such events may be sombre or celebratory, they may be relatively unobtrusive or vigorous social events with guest lists, invitations and professional musicians hired to perform before friends, relatives – and ancestors. Either way, the events and sites associated with the dead are reported even by the more casual of observers, and even by those otherwise unaware that Madagascar is well known in the anthropological literature for its funerary practice.

Throughout what has become an extensive body of documentation of Malagasy custom the theme of second burial constantly emerges as a distinctive feature. It is sufficiently rare a practice elsewhere in the world for its presence in Madagascar to be of considerable interest. Its essential characteristic is the phasing of funerary rites so that the deceased will be exhumed some time after a preliminary burial and the process of entombment completed. What is often overlooked in discussion of this practice, however, is that it is by no means general in Madagascar. Funerary customs, in fact, are extremely complex and varied and there is very considerable divergence over many points of detail, not merely over the definitive character of any particular burial. Thus, while actual interment may occur in some places, amongst the Betsimisaraka, the Tanala and the Antankarana, the coffin is simply placed on top of the ground. The Mahafaly and Antandroy for their part construct their tombs by piling up stones. Coffins themselves are not universal; a simple shroud may suffice. Whether the body is disposed of quickly or laid out for a period, whether burial takes place by day or night, whether corpses are kept singly or grouped – variations of this kind may well imply significant differences in ideas about the process of burial and the nature of the transitions involved.

At least one indication of this is the fact that the procedures frequently

Washing feet in flowing water after a visit to a tomb. The act is one which follows contact with the potentially polluting materials associated with the dead. Antaimoro.

differ for burying sovereigns and their subjects. In the east and south-east of the island, for instance, the death of a 'king' is not announced and no general ceremony takes place. The death is kept secret for as long as possible. The body is taken by night at the earliest opportunity and placed in the tomb by members of the royal lineage. In the case of the Antaisaka the name of the ruler is changed at his decease and he is never after death referred to by the name he bore whilst alive. Local explanation of this divergence from usual practice points to the importance of avoiding disputes over succession and of concealing from potential enemies the temporary interruption in leadership occasioned by a royal death. The death of persons already regarded as more than mortal poses problems in a system geared to coping with transitions between the merely human and the ancestral.

The pollution of death

Clearly it is not possible here to survey and interpret all the many divergencies in practice across the whole island. A general descriptive account drawn from many of the available sources has already been published (Decary 1962), and a number of more sophisticated discussions of particular traditions have been published (for example, Bloch 1971, Huntingdon 1973, Huntingdon and Metcalf 1979). However, it is possible to locate some of the underlying themes and see how they may produce different varieties of funerary practice.

It is instructive to examine the burial practice of a people called Vazimba, who lived along the banks of the river Manambolo in western Madagascar in what is now Sakalava country. These Vazimba (a term used generically, of early or original occupants of a particular territory) no longer exist as a distinctive group and the practice outlined is now submerged in the broader complexity of Sakalava burials. The account is that of the early French authority Alfred Grandidier (1891, pp. 310–11):

> After having washed the corpse and clothed it in its finest garments, they place it in a squatting posture upon the *kibany* (a bed or couch), and as if it were still living; and the relatives or friends attend it night and day, talking to it, putting into its hand a spoon, full of rice or any other kind of food, etc. Formerly the liquids produced by the decomposition of the flesh were taken to a special place, which was sprinkled with the blood of an ox in order to nourish the *fananina* or snake, which they believe to be produced from these putrid liquids. Since the conquest of the country by the Sakalava king Lahifotsy, these customs have been to some extent abandoned, and as soon as the effluvium becomes too offensive, the corpse is buried. But, at the end of about a year, they take it out of the ground and wash the bones, which are placed in a new coffin, and are then buried for good and all.

This account no doubt has historical interest in itself, although it would hardly be feasible to try and derive other traditions from it merely because it relates the customs of one of the older communities of Malagasy settlement. What is more illuminating is that it shows a tradition apparently at a moment of change, of reappraisal, when more basic concerns are asses-

A Betsimisaraka cemetry. The coffins themselves are simply set on the ground. Nowadays a roof of corrugated iron is usually erected as protection, although overhanging rocks may also be used as shelter. From Sibree 1896, p. 290.

sed. In particular, it describes second burial – the bones of the deceased Vazimba are recovered, washed and then re-interred in a final resting-place. Grandidier further implies that this may not have been original practice but an innovation forced on them by the numerically and militarily superior Sakalava, apparently disgusted by the stench of unburied corpses. Interestingly, the 'innovation' would not have been merely imitative or imposed upon them, for the Sakalava do not themselves practise exhumation of the dead. Whether or not this actually represents an innovation in Vazimba tradition might be open to debate; the significant point, however, is that it could have been. Because second burial is often a highly conspicuous event in those parts of Madagascar where it occurs and because it is not generally so overtly practised elsewhere in the world, it is easy to assume that when it does occur it marks a significant divergence of tradition. Grandidier's text illustrates neatly that a more fundamental concern underlies Malagasy burial customs, a concern with impurity and with the polluting character of putrid material. Single and secondary burials can both be so structured as to accommodate this notion and one can merge into the other.

Details of funerary practice across the island make clear how crucial is this concept. It has two aspects. One concerns the actions taken by persons who come into contact with the dead or with things and places associated with death. Those who have touched polluted materials, who have, for instance, dressed a corpse, are obliged to purify themselves. Touch (*tohina*) is said to be sufficient to impart impurity. Its transmission, however, need not even require actual physical contact. It is enough to have visited the house in which a body is laid out, to attend a burial, or visit a tomb, to risk contamination. Further, to smell rotting or putrid substances is also potentially polluting, as the Vazimba case shows. Smell (*fofona*) denotes an actual emanation and can be used of vapour as well as of smell; in other words it is physical. In some places, where bodies are not disposed of shortly after death, incense may be used not just to conceal but to 'purify' the immediate environment in which it is placed. Anyone who nevertheless smells polluted materials will spit constantly to rid themselves of the pollution inhaled. For those who have actually touched a body or otherwise been associated with death, washing, both of the person and of clothes, removes the contagion. The washing should preferably take place in flowing water to disperse the pollution.

The second feature of funerary customs which is relevant here is the disposal of materials associated with the deceased, meaning both personal items formerly in the possession of the dead and most importantly the rotted flesh of the body itself, the most polluting element of all. Many graves in Madagascar have around them a whole range of discarded objects – cups, plates, spoons, hats, umbrellas, zips and combs, even sometimes chairs or tables piled up on the grave itself. These are not necessarily placed there to 'furnish' or render familiar in some mystical sense the new abode of the deceased; they are also left there as materials which in being associated with the dead have become polluting in themselves. Alternatively they may be burnt. In Betsimisaraka tradition, for example, it is the practice to burn the last abode of a deceased person. This may be a complete house with its belongings or, if someone is known to be near death, they may be taken and placed in the shade of a tree and this, in due course, will be set alight. In one instance at a hospital in south-eastern Madagascar the patients disposed of all the bedding and medical equipment from the ward when one of their number died. It is equally common to burn or to leave at the graveside the bier or any other equipment used to transport the body to the tomb, and which has thereby become polluted.

The liquids produced by the decomposition of the flesh, however, are the crucial agent of impurity and must be carefully handled and disposed

Merina women with hair undone as a mark of mourning for the dead. By the Malagasy artist Rainimaharosoa.

of. Some estimate of the time it takes for the process of dissolution of the corpse is one of the most important markers in determining the phasing of funerary rites. Methods of preserving the body found elsewhere – mummification, for instance – very rarely occur in Madagascar and then only to exceptional people; nor is the body itself disposed of through cremation, although materials associated with the dead may be burnt. In principle the process of decomposition takes place unimpeded, but the progress is charted in burial procedures. The aim is to finish up with the clean, dry bones of the deceased. It is these which are ultimately the subject of final burial, and in so far as the idea of the ancestors is represented materially, it is located in these bones and in the family or clan tomb in which they are placed.

Single and second burial

The two versions of Vazimba-Sakalava burial illustrate the two basic ways of achieving these results. In one the body is kept; the materials of decomposition are collected; and these and the skeletal remains are buried separately. In the other the corpse is buried almost immediately; the process of dissolution takes place unseen, in a temporary grave; and the bones are subsequently exhumed, washed and placed in a permanent ancestral tomb. Both techniques produce the same result: the separation of polluting 'wet' materials from 'dry', 'sacred' ones, the bones of the ancestors. In both cases, too, the bones are ultimately collected together in a communal tomb. The idea that funerary rites might be so staged and have these symbolic dimensions was already foreshadowed for anthropologists in Hertz 1907. Here it is worth emphasising that while to the observer the process of second burial may seem the most dramatic realisation of the principles involved in this separation of flesh and bone, the process of keeping and watching the corpse embodies similar ideas. No doubt burying and exhuming the body perhaps several years later ensures that the corpse is more completely skeletal at the point when it is taken to the ancestral burial-ground. The time-lapse also enables the event to be a more elaborate one, for it is a considerable financial undertaking which may require the raising of significantly large resources amongst a group of possibly dispersed kinsmen. Nevertheless, the alternative practice of keeping the dead in a village amongst the living whilst decomposition takes place certainly extended to months in the past, whatever the inconveniences involved.

These two alternative methods of treating the dead correspond to particular traditions: the first is broadly that of some of the Betsimisaraka group and of their southerly neighbours, while the second with its emphasis on reburial is typically that of the Merina and the Betsileo in the centre of the island. Other traditions can be similarly located within this broad model. Perhaps the most divergent practice is that found in the south-east of the island, an area which is also less fully documented than other regions. However, the polluting nature of the materials of decomposition is clearly still a concern. The Antaimanambondro, for example, bury the dead shortly after their decease and while flesh and body are still intact. Burial takes place at the traditional communal graves (*kibori*) located some distance from villages. These graves are designed on a pattern familiar in the southeast, that of trenches in which kinsmen who in life were of the same status and gender are buried together. Clearly for those worried about the fate of polluting materials this poses a potential problem for there is an obvious risk of contaminating the other skeletal remains and bones already housed there. To overcome this difficulty the Antaimanambondro dig up all the

Cotton textile used as a burial shroud
(*lamba mena*), the border decorated
with metal beads. Betsileo. W. 142 cm.
BM 1928–58. Field Museum, Chicago.

remains in a particular trench so that the most recently deceased are placed at the bottom of the grave with the older bones replaced above, Decompositon can therefore occur without fear of polluting other ancestral remains.

No doubt the exhumations involved could be interpreted as a form of second burial, but it is not at all clear that the bones are the subject of any special treatment on such occasions. The procedure seems largely to be a matter of finding a practical solution to a particular problem. The Antaisaka (of whom the Antaimanambondro are usually considered to be part) hold instead an annual ceremony at which those who have died in the intervening year are honoured. Only when this has taken place are the dead considered to have been fully admitted to the *kibori*. The ceremony, although it involves no actual inspection of the bones, retains the phasing of events which is characteristic of Malagasy funerals and the timing is such that the separation of flesh from bone is already advanced.

The Antaimanambondro do not make coffins but instead envelop the body in a mat or in cloth. This, like the use of other mortuary artefacts, is no doubt essentially a matter of local tradition. However, since the disposal of the liquids of decomposition is of considerable cultural interest throughout Madagascar when and how shrouds or coffins are used are important questions. Clearly coffins, in so far as they act to contain polluted materials, can best be used as a final receptacle in which to house the dead, brought into play once decomposition is over. Since the Antaimanambondro do not use coffins, the liquids can escape harmlessly into the earth. Where the recently dead are placed in coffins, they will be dispensed with

73

or replaced at any subsequent phase of burial practice since to do otherwise would leave incomplete the separation of polluted materials from the skeleton.

There is, however, at least one important exception to this general rule. This is, or rather was, the tradition of Merina royal burial. The practice of constructing a coffin of melted-down silver coinage was introduced for the burial of Andrianampoinimerina in 1810 and continued by his successors up to the time of Ranavalona II. (Ranavalona III, having been exiled by the French, died in Algiers and with her death all remnants of the tradition and the monarchy itself were at an end.) The coffin of Andrianampoinimerina was placed in a large wooden 'canoe' of a type which had itself formerly served as a royal coffin. The burial was concluded within a matter of weeks and was followed by no procedure of second burial or other reshrouding of the remains. The body too was placed in an individual rather than a collective tomb. In this instance, therefore, no ritual acknowledgement of the physical changes that come with death is made and its powerful symbolism remains unexploited.

The secrecy of royal death in some parts and the uniqueness of royal funerary rites imply that people of high ritual status cannot, like mere mortals, dissolve into polluted and polluting substances, or that their condition as influential ancestors might be impaired by contact with such material. Their death, after all, may be deliberately hidden, their funerary rites conducted by night and in secret, as in the south-east of the island; they may (in the exceptional case of the chiefs of the Antankarana) be subjects of rudimentary mummification; or they may be buried intact, in coffins, and never thereafter moved. Although the last of these practices is the familiar anticipated method of burial in the Christian tradition, for the Merina, and particularly in the period before the arrival of missionaries, the implications would have been striking and unavoidable – only someone immune to contamination or exempt from the normal processes of decomposition would remain unpolluted by such a burial.

Famadihana

One effect of the rules governing the burial of the Merina sovereign was that royal remains, unlike those of everyone else in Imerina, were not the subject of *famadihana*, possibly the best-known feature of Malagasy tradition in general but essentially a Merina ceremony and one which continues to be important up to the present day. *Famadihana* are sometimes described as if they were simply a burial procedure, but the ceremony is much more than simply the final stage in an individual's funerary rites. *Famadihana* may take place when the remains of someone who died in a distant place, probably several years previously, are returned to the ancestral tomb. This is the most frequent reason for the event in Imerina (Bloch 1971, p. 145ff.). It may also, however, provide an occasion for other corpses already placed in the tomb to be taken out, treated, and returned to the sepulchre, or this may take place separately with no additional corpse to be incorporated into the tomb. *Famadihana* may also be performed when a new tomb is inaugurated and bodies are brought from temporary burials for inclusion

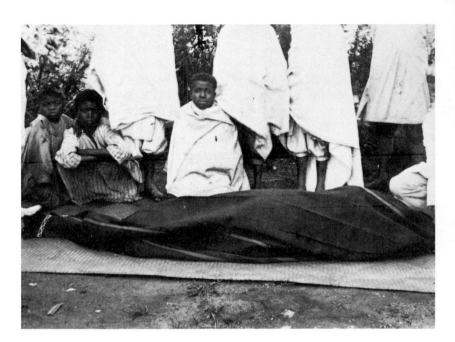

Corpse wrapped in its appropriate burial shroud (*lamba mena*) prior to being re-entombed. Merina.

Two bodies rewrapped in their shrouds and carried on biers being returned to the ancestral tomb after a *famadihana*. The 'mourners' are dressed in the appropriate Malagasy colour – white. Merina.

with ancestral remains moved from the old tomb to the new. This is the principal occasion for the ceremony amongst the Betsileo, to the south of Imerina, who also practise it (Kottak 1980, p. 229).

Famadihana literally means 'turning the dead'. The essential act is the rewrapping of the corpse in fresh silk shrouds, *lamba mena*. The event always takes place during the day. The tomb is opened and any remains which are to be rewrapped are first placed in a mat together with any rotted shroud that may still surround the body. Not infrequently a number of corpses may be taken out on the same occasion. To the accompaniment of music, dancing and singing – including, in one report (*A Glance at Madagascar* 1973), a spirited rendering of 'Roll out the Barrel' – and in a general atmosphere of festivity the remains are brought to the village. Here a celebration takes place. The body is carried or held, talked to by its descendants, danced with, and taken, perhaps, on a tour of the locality where any new developments might be pointed out. When the body is rewrapped in its new cloth, the old rotted shroud is left in place. If, however, all that remains of the body are bones, these will be washed. Before dusk, arrayed in a new shroud and having been thoroughly fêted for a day, the body is returned to the tomb and the entrance sealed up again until the next *famadihana* is arranged.

Every Merina, even if no longer living in the deme of his ancestors, would wish to have his body returned for incorporation into the ancestral tomb. Only the sovereign in the past was exempt from the fear of being buried in isolation. Equally every member of the deme, however distantly they may have lived, would anticipate making a contribution to the upkeep of the tomb itself, and to the not inconsiderable cost of holding a *famadihana*. This is not mere sentimentality; the most abiding interpretation of the purpose of *famadihana*, that of Maurice Bloch (1971, and developed in subsequent publications), emphasises both the regrouping of corpses, which is involved in gathering together the bodies of dispersed kinsmen in one tomb, and also the reshuffling of these remains which the *famadihana* process produces. In other words, although individual dead may be remembered for a time and their remains are identifiable as a separate shrouded corpse, gradually the memory of them becomes intermingled with that of the family ancestors in general, just as physically their bones become grouped with those of deceased kinsmen in the tomb itself. Maintaining and ensuring the common housing of ancestral remains in the common sepulchre is seen, Bloch argues, as essential to receiving ancestral blessing. Indeed, more than that, the act of regrouping the dead in *famadihana* itself leads to ancestral blessing. It is not just that being buried alone leads to a lonely and uncertain death; it also impairs the flow of vitality from ancestors to living kinsmen, throwing into doubt the fate of the whole group.

It is interesting to note, finally, that amongst the other main techniques of attracting ancestral blessing one, spirit possession, also frequently involves the wearing of shrouds. Feeley-Harnik in a compelling discussion (forthcoming) draws attention to the practice of Sakalava spirit mediums to shroud themselves like corpses in order that royal spirits may speak out. She makes the point that shrouding, whether in reburial rituals or in spirit possession, induces speech; it renews and revitalises.

Tombs and cenotaphs

Antaimoro cemetery in the village of Ivato, the 'houses' of the dead separated from those of the living only by a rough wood fence. The triangular structure above the house in the foreground duplicates a house nearby in which the *mpanjaka* (or 'king') holds audience. This one is for aristocratic burials.

So far little has been said about any metaphysical ideas that might be tied up in Malagasy notions of death and in customs and ceremonies associated with the dead. The anthropologist Hertz made much of the concept of 'spirit' as basic to any proposed understanding of the various changes which the corpse undergoes and their expression in the symbolism of funerary practice. However, neither here, nor in the more general literature on Malagasy burial, is there much reference to such things as the fate of the 'soul', the transmigration of the 'spirit', or, indeed, to the nature and circumstances of an afterlife. It is only when a body is *not* for whatever reason incorporated into an ancestral tomb that there is any precision about what might happen to it (this, no doubt, adding force to the ultimate punishment for wrong-doing, that of exclusion from the tomb). Generally it is held that those dead deliberately subject to a solitary burial are somehow transformed into a bat, the cat-like *fosa*, or some other dread creature of the wild. Only amongst some of the Betsimisaraka is there reported to be any more general association between the 'spirits' of the dead and any other living entity – in this case the *babakoto*, the largest of the lemurs, which is as a result singled out by local tradition as a preserved species. Even here, however, the concepts involved are hardly explicit.

The tomb and the house

There is, nevertheless, some notion of an afterlife in Malagasy thought, however hazy. This is already implied in the universal belief in the power of ancestral action, the capacity to bless and give vitality, to render efficacious and to cure. Furthermore, the dead do have an address: the afterlife is lived out in and from the tomb or some designated and related site. This image of an address, of the tomb as the 'residence' of the dead, is sometimes quite explicit. The ruling clans of the Antaimoro, for instance, formerly erected as tombs wooden houses in the same form as those of the living and located in the village occupied by the living separated off only by a fence. Inside the houses trenches were excavated beneath the flooring to act as graves and the dead grouped within according to their status, age and gender. Personal belongings of the deceased were placed in the house-tomb as they would be were the dwelling occcupied. At the village of Ivato near Vohipeno a collection of these Antaimoro 'houses of the dead' still survives.

Tombs, however, have also shown a more recent tendency to evolve in style and form, especially as part of the changes associated with the introduction of cement as a building material. Typically this has been used to construct not only houses but, most importantly, tombs. There are few parts of the island where the durability of this new material has not been exploited, often giving rise to a sharp contrast between the strength and permanence of tombs and the often fragile impermanent character of human dwellings. The contrast is not inappropriate: Andrianampoinimerina is himself credited with a remark to the effect that dwelling on earth is no more than a voyage, but dwelling in a tomb is for eternity. The developments have included a movement towards more house-like forms and, for catechists, tombs with a deliberately church-like appearance.

These cement structures often replace what were formerly stone-built tombs. Those of the Merina and Betsileo are among the more fully described. Merina tombs are substantial rectangular structures made of uncut dry stone which rise to perhaps 3 m or so above the surface of the ground and may cover an area of maybe 50 sq m. Large slabs of stone form the door and the roof, which was, in the case of higher-ranked demes, sometimes topped by a small model house known as *trano manara* ('cold house'). The external surrounds of the door are frequently decorated with a mixture of floral or geometric designs in relief, a practice originally inspired by Jean Laborde in the latter half of the nineteenth century. These tombs are also subterranean so that, descending into the sepulchre, an underground

A royal Merina tomb in the courtyard of the palace at Antananarivo.

The tomb of a Betsimisaraka catechist with, behind, the corrugated iron roof protecting coffins laid out in the more traditional manner on the surface of the ground.

Traditional form of Merina tomb with its massive stone door and relief decoration, a practice introduced in the 19th century. From Sibree 1915, p. 118.

chamber is entered which has stone shelving arranged in tiers to receive the shrouded corpses. Many Betsileo tombs are constructed in a similar manner, although nobility here were sometimes buried in deep underground caves the entrance to which would be walled off, a custom the Bara continue to observe. The excavated chambers beneath Betsileo graves are often substantial, but they lack the structure of shelving which characterises Merina tombs and instead the dead are laid out on matting. Betsileo also, among a number of variants, build tombs from ground level upwards with no underground cavity. These they call simply *trano vato* ('houses of stone').

The tombs of southern Madagascar are, however, the most spectacular of the island's stone-built funerary sites. Those of the Antandroy, for example, attain lengths of up to some 50 m on each of their four sides, the size and degree of elaboration being in large measure related to the standing of the deceased in whose honour they are erected. All are made of local stone, but normally they include, centred on facing sides of the rectangular structure, two enormous upright stone slabs, the *vatolahy* and *vatovavy* ('male and female stones'). The tomb is completed with the usual range of possessions associated with the deceased and large numbers of cattle skulls, often well over 100, preserved from the feasting which has taken place at the interment and throughout the process of building the tomb. These are in addition testimony to the wealth of the family as expressed in their herds.

The inside of a Merina tomb with deme members perched ready to receive a rewrapped corpse. The decorative stonework of the outside faces of the tomb is repeated inside.

The more westerly groups of Antandroy also occasionally include carved figures or wood poles surmounted by some representational image on their tombs. This, however, is a practice they have learnt from the neighbouring Mahafaly, some Antandroy clans having bought the right to use such images from the Mahafaly kings. The distinctive Mahafaly post is composed of alternating geometric motifs sometimes supported on a carved human figure and usually with a sculpted scene of some kind at the top, often drawn from everyday experience. In principle the use of such funeray posts is restricted to the members of noble clans and to clan heads on whose graves up to sixteen or more such posts may be employed. The Mahafaly and, in their more limited manner, the Antandroy are not, however, alone in their traditions of sculpture on monuments to the dead. The Sakalava,

Sihanaka and Antanosy also have such traditions, as in a minor way do (or did) the Bara and the Antaimoro.

The siting of tombs

The contrasts here are already striking in terms simply of the external form and style of tombs, whether of stone or cement or, like Betsimisaraka graves, cemeteries of wood coffins laid out on the ground with only a rudimentary roof or overhanging rock for protection. Some tombs are highly decorative, others simple. Some are truly collective family or clan mausoleums; yet like those of the Antandroy or of pre-eminent persons in other traditions they can sometimes be single burials. A further distinction in Malagasy practice which carries with it broader implications is that between tombs which are visible, accessible and approachable, and those which are deliberately hidden and perhaps rarely visited or seen.

Thus Merina tombs, for example, although not necessarily sited for maximum visibility, are not in any way concealed. They are constructed within the deme, on ancestral land (*tanindrazana*) to whose fertility the ancestors

The older form of Antandroy tomb with stone sides and large standing stones at its edges. The two sculptures appear to be cenotaphs in the style of the Antanosy sculptor Fesira.

whose bones lie inside are regarded as essential. Usually they will be placed outside the village boundary, but in special circumstances they might be located within the settlement thus imitating royal tombs which were sited within the palace itself (Bloch 1981, p. 139). Furthermore, the process of regrouping bodies, of carrying out, on occasion, special *famadihanas*, means that they are frequently visited and often opened. They are 'lived with'; where there is a village or a deme there are always, in the same territory, tombs.

In a similar way the tombs of the Antandroy are readily visible structures. The land in which they are located is admittedly flat and vegetation sparse so that even the long low tombs they typically construct would be difficult to hide completely if that were the intention. Yet the erection of massive upright stones, the *vatolahy* and the *vatovavy*, ensure that they are always prominently visible. Betsileo country, on the other hand, is much hillier and provides better opportunity to locate tombs in discreet places. Frequently, however, they are placed on the skyline which emphasises their presence.

Practice varies somewhat, but there is a clear contrast between these examples of conspicuous tombs and the traditions of the Betsimisaraka and some of their near neighbours in the south-east of the island. Here tombs tend to be sited in sacred groves, often at some distance from places of habitation. The presence of such sites is predictable only in some cases by virtue of the increasing impenetrability of the vegetation in what may already be thickly forested country. In such instances it may often be taboo to cut back the undergrowth in the area of a tomb. Access is strictly controlled and only to be had by reference to a ritual specialist, who is responsible for ensuring that only the appropriate dead are buried there and also that the motives of any living person wishing to visit a funerary site are acceptable. Usually such a visit can be made only under his personal supervision.

The extreme case is that of the Antaimanambondro. Their centre today is the large village of Manambondro which lies on the river Manambondro some distance from its estuary on the south-eastern coast. The basin of the river provides fertile land for cultivation and it is here that many smaller settlements are located. The Antaimanambondro practise the tradition of collective burial, and their graves are located down river in the marshy lands adjacent to the estuary. Access is most readily had by canoe, for no path is regularly maintained to the site; indeed, the graves themselves are not cleaned or kept up in a systematic fashion. This is done only when the graves are visited for the purposes of burial. Anyone found visiting the graveyard at any other time would immediately be suspected of sorcery.

There is, however, a major difficulty associated with maintaining such a system of severely limited access. After all, where the dead are buried quickly and access to the site of the grave is irregular, little apparent room is left for any cultural recognition of the separation of flesh from bone which is so characteristic a feature of Malagasy practice. The Antaimanambondro, of course, are careful to place the recently dead at the bottom of the burial so as not to 'pollute' other bodies placed there, which is at least some acknowledgement of the symbolic significance of bodily decomposition. Nevertheless, the opportunity provided by a new interment to reshroud or wash other bones already in the burial does not seem to be taken up. The Antaimanambondro, however, like the Antanosy to their south, have one distinctive practice which marks them out from other groups and which adds a further dimension to what would otherwise be a swift and, in Malagasy terms, truncated method of disposing of the dead: both peoples erect what can be very substantial memorial sites in close proximity to their villages.

Cenotaphs and burials

Cenotaphs are common in Madagascar. They are usually upright standing stones which are called by a variety of names, the commonest being *vato*

The lines of cement obelisks and standing stones with tall wooden poles to which are attached the skulls of sacrificed cattle. An elaborate Antaimanambondro memorial site in south-east Madagascar.

mitsangana ('standing stone') and *vatolahy* ('male stone'). They may be adorned in various ways – sometimes with white cloth (white, not black, being in parts of Madagascar, as in the Far East, the colour of mourning), or they may be furnished with a wood frame to which the skulls of sacrificed cattle are attached. They may commemorate events or they may commemorate the dead. If their function is the latter, they are put up when there is no body to bury, if, for example, someone has drowned and the remains were not recovered, or if someone dies far from home. In such instances the erection of the memorial stone often at the burial-site itself might be seen as a means of reuniting the family dead when this is not otherwise possible.

In the case of the Antaimanambondro and the Antanosy, however, there is a further dimension, for both do bury their dead, yet some time later they create separate memorials to each deceased person. These may be upright stones or in modern times they might be cement obelisks. Furthermore, with the Antaimanambondro the alignment of these cenotaphs appears to reproduce horizontally the relationships between corpses in their vertical graves. Individual lines of standing stones seem to commemorate those buried in the same trench-like grave, and often poles with the skulls of sacrificed cattle attached complete the site. It is therefore a kind of visible and visual representation of the burial-site itself where the bodies are unseen beneath the earth and the cemetery concealed and access forbidden to visitors other than to bury or be buried. These sites can, in fact, be quite near villages, and Antanosy burial-grounds, far from being in remote inaccessible places, are often close to human habitations hidden perhaps by a nearby thicket of trees. What this suggests is that the separation of the graves from the village, the burial-ground from the memorial site, is import-

83

ant and not simply a question of, for example, villages having moved to new sites some distance from ancestral places of burial.

It is more instructive perhaps to see the erection of these stones and the placing of cattle horns not only as the creation of memorials but as the completion of funerary rites. In the same way when there is no body to bury the creation of memorials completes a process of burial begun elsewhere. In some cases the kind of substitution involved is quite explicit: the Antaisaka, for example (amongst whom the Antaimanambondro are frequently numbered), call the memorial stone *solopati* (literally 'substitute corpse'), and its ceremonial emplacement follows the form of funerary rites.

According to this interpretation the building of cenotaphs emerges as an equivalent to the second burial practised elsewhere. Antaimanambondro avoid graves because they are places of pollution; the separation of flesh from bone has not taken place when corpses are buried there, and, since it is polluted earth, only sorcerers could be interested in the substances found in such a place. The creation of the cenotaph some time later and some distance away acknowledges that in the distant grave the flesh has left the bone. On the cenotaph are displayed bones which a similar process of decompositon has rendered 'dry', the skulls of cattle sacrificed in honour of, and here to represent, the ancestors. The cenotaph is in this sense like the tomb of the Merina or the Betsileo: it is the place associated with purified ancestors and, like the tombs familiar from the plateau, it need not be hidden but can be 'lived with'.

Where then do Antandroy tombs fit in? After all, it is only the Antandroy and the neighbouring Mahafaly who are noted amongst Malagasy for displaying cattle skulls on *tombs* as opposed to cenotaphs. If the skulls of sacrificed cattle are a reference to the condition of ancestral bones, there is little point in displaying them if through either second burial or exposing the body flesh has been seen to leave the bone. Thus the Bara, for example, practise second burial and do not make overt use of cattle skulls on tombs. When there is no body to bury, however, they erect stones in some highly visible place to which the skulls of cattle are attached. The restriction of skulls to cenotaphs rather than tombs and to circumstances where burial is otherwise incomplete is fairly consistent in Madagascar.

The usual interpretation of the numerous skulls seen on the tombs of southern Madagascar is that they are proclamations of the wealth and status of the dead as of their surviving relatives, for the cattle slaughtered are drawn from the family herds and the size of such herds is a measure of family success. However, there is more to it than this, and indeed Antandroy tradition has certain similarities to that in the south-east. Burial takes place shortly after death. The body is taken to the burial-site and interred. Thereafter the process of constructing the tomb begins on top of the ground in which the burial has taken place. To this extent, although there may well be varieties of practice, the tomb need not contain the body at all, but is rather built on top of it. Its construction could be interpreted as part of the funerary process in a similar fashion to the creation of cenotaphs in the south-east.

It takes several months to complete the larger tombs during which time

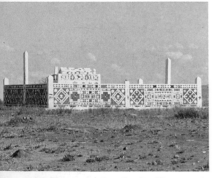

Modern Antandroy tomb with cement-finished sides and painted designs. These have developed out of an older tradition in which the cut stones dressing the side of the tomb were often arranged by size and shape to produce patterning.

those responsible for its construction set up temporary camp at the site. At the end of the period a series of events which are associated with the final stages of funerary rites elsewhere on the island take place. The completed tomb has placed on it the cattle skulls marking the 'dryness' of the remains which in the interim have gone through the process of decomposition unseen in the ground beneath the ever-mounting stone structure. Furthermore, the completed monument has facing each other at either side of the tomb the two large standing stones, *vatolahy* and *vatovavy*. It is possible that their siting is a further reference to the separation of flesh from bone, for ideas of male and female are associated with bone and flesh in other parts of the island – for instance, amongst the Bara immediately to the north (Huntingdon 1973).

The making of ancestors, then, involves charting the stages of change through which the body passes at death. There are a great variety of mortuary customs found in Madagascar, much greater than is often apparent in discussions of Malagasy funerary practice. However, three models by which this process of decomposition is delineated in Malagasy burials have been identified. In the first the body is in principle disposed of quickly in a temporary grave; after an interval of time it is recovered and the bones incorporated in a collective family tomb. In the second the body is exposed at death and left for a lengthy period during which the liquid of decomposition is collected. This and the dry corpse are subjects of separate burial. Finally, the body may be disposed of quickly, a monument subsequently created whether a tomb or more strictly a cenotaph, and cattle skulls, evocative of the dryness of the dead, placed upon it. Whichever method is adopted, the emphasis is always the same – the need to generate a dry non-polluted corpse which is essential to maintaining a well-disposed family of ancestors.

The ancestral shrine (*fisokina*) in a Betsimisaraka village. Tombs are traditionally located in the forests and caves at some distance from villages. *Fisokina* are thus erected as ancestral sites within areas of human occupation at which sacrifice and other ceremonies take place.

Funerary sculpture

Some funerary sculpture is directly commemorative in character, whereas in other cases the intention seems rather to be that of reflecting aspects of the symbolism of the mortuary process itself. Some images appear on cenotaphs properly speaking, but more often perhaps they are placed on tombs, even though they may, nevertheless, serve some more general commemorative purpose. The subjects may be human or may include birds, animals and manufactured objects such as aeroplanes and motor cars, sometimes as part of some more complex scene.

All the sculpture examined here is in wood, although cement sculpture, either in relief on the side of funerary monuments, or as an object in its own right, is beginning to become familiar, particularly in southern Madagascar. Indeed, with the exception of the Sihanaka in the north-east of the plateau, all the traditions of funerary sculpture that have been documented occur in the south and west of the island. This is perhaps predictable. After all, these are areas where second burial is not found. Commemorative sculpture, in so far as it isolates and honours individuals,

Mahafaly tomb of a noble family showing the range of subjects traditional on *aloalo* interspersed amongst the cattle horns on the top of the tomb.

emphasises particular deceased relatives as opposed to the community of ancestors. Second burial, however, and especially the *famadihana* process in grouping and reshuffling ancestral bones moves more in the direction of the anonymity of the dead. This is most evident in the case of the Merina where it has been stressed that the tomb is so regarded that over time individual dead housed within it merge conceptually with the tomb itself: 'The focus is shifted from an actual person, whether alive or dead, to a non-individuated ancestor, and then to a thing – the tomb' (Bloch 1971, p. 122). The Merina traditionally make no funerary sculpture.

There is in Malagasy no single word by which to distinguish sculpture, either as a general category of object or specifically as a funerary artefact. Those terms that are available are all compounds of the word *sary*, which has the general meaning of 'an image'. However, the term *aloalo* has gained some currency in some of the art books where it is often used as if it were generic. *Aloalo* comes from the word *alo* which carries with it the sense of an intermediary or messenger (Decary 1962, p. 278). It therefore refers to the function rather than the form of an object, so that not all sculpture found in association with burials is necessarily *aloalo* and not all *aloalo* are necessarily sculptural. The term has been taken over from the Mahafaly, amongst whom it refers to one specific form of funerary object, and has been extended to other objects where its use may be inappropriate.

Aloalo are strictly the polar sculptures referred to above which certain royal Mahafaly clans reserved to their own use. They have been the subject of a number of preliminary field studies, and the sites in which they occur are well photographed and recorded. Yet few who have studied them have felt able to venture any conclusive interpretation of their significance (Boulfroy 1976, Woulkoff 1976, and, as a more general survey, Decary 1951 and 1962). Furthermore, whatever their original intent, this may well have altered for not only have the rights to the use of *aloalo* been extended but the form of the *aloalo* itself has evolved.

The classic style associated with the older tombs is a single naked figure with, above, the projection already referred to with its geometric motifs topped usually by a carved zebu or bird. In more recent times, however, the style has developed to the point where a whole series of scenes and images are now employed. Among the newer motifs are cyclists and horse-riders, aeroplanes and *taxi-brousse*, gendarmes arresting thieves or sorcerers, a colonial judge, hunters and warriors, drinkers, or a funeral cortège. What this suggests is a shift of emphasis from the earlier forms of funerary sculpture which all appear to comment on the kinds of transition involved in burial practice – in this they resemble the funerary sculpture of some of the Sakalava. The later sculpture, however, in referring to events associated with the dead are more directly commemorative and as such are more comparable to the cenotaphs of the Antanosy and particularly the remarkable series of memorial sculptures dating from the 1930s and 40s and attributed to the prolific and gifted Antanosy sculptor Fesira.

Sakalava tombs are varied reflecting both the diverse origins of the Sakalava themselves and hierarchical divisions within their society. Royalty possess spirit mediums at their death and in this respect retain

Mahafaly *aloalo* displaying a number of scenes recalling the life of the deceased and resulting in a highly complex sculpture.

Female figure with child in the Sakalava style and from a Vezo tomb. H. (of figure) 90 cm. MAA 63–2–215.

a bodily incarnation. Their tombs are not perhaps as vital a focus for their descendants or subjects as their continuing spiritual existence expressed in the person of a medium and certain royal relics. Funerary sculpture is hardly relevant since in a sense royalty do not die but represent themselves through invading a living person. Sculpture is in fact used on the tombs of certain higher-ranking groups of Sakalava rather than on royal tombs which are by contrast modest (Bloch 1981). The subjects of this sculpture are again, as those of the Mahafaly, naked figures and birds represented singly or, in the case of the Sakalava, in erotic embrace. Two features in particular distinguish Sakalava figurative work: one is the exaggeration of the sexual organs, and the other is the predominance of the female which, where a contrast with a male figure is made, is carved on a larger scale.

Any notion that these figures commemorate the dead on whose graves they appear, or more particularly that they are portraits, would certainly seem to be out of the question. For all Malagasy the wearing of clothing is a strictly observed habit, even in the warmest parts of the island. Nudity, when it is inadvertently encountered, is always startling and embarrassing. Washing or bathing is carried out discreetly; it is only between sexual partners that nudity is admitted, and in other contexts is a mark of madness. The dead too are in principle always clothed. Thus when the corpse is washed it is only by and in the presence of people who should usually be relatives of the deceased and of the same sex. Equally, clothing and shrouding the dead are the very acts which assert the proper quality of regard in which the living hold the dead. Clothing sculpture in fact was common amongst the Sihanaka and Antaimoro. There is little doubt, then, that the nudity of the Sakalava and Mahafaly funerary figures implies sexuality itself rather than necessarily the sexuality of particular persons. Indeed, amongst taboos associated with those graves where such sculpture is displayed is a ban on their being visited at the same time by persons between whom there are incest prohibitions.

Most discussions of Sakalava sculpture have either missed these points or confined themselves to some general statement about death and regeneration, as if they were rather specifically Sakalava ideas. Certainly in carving female figures more prominently than male, and thereby asserting the priority of Sakalava women, some notion of rebirth is arguably implicit in the sculpture. However, Mahafaly graves in displaying naked figures imply sexuality *per se*, and it is striking that many events, funerary or otherwise – at ceremonies associated with the birth of the New Year, for example – were in the past exceptional times when unrestricted sexuality was stressed, whether actually or by implication.

In the Sakalava case the implication is certainly there, for even if single figures are put up they generally face each other, male confronting female, across a square structure. It has been remarked (Lombard 1973, p.96) that this arrangement draws on the *vintana* system described above. A male figure placed in the north-east facing a female one on the south-west replicates a situation which is taboo. Persons with opposing *vintana* as determined by time of birth and its related spatial reference would not in normal circumstances knowingly engage in such a relationship.

Sakalava tomb.

Sakalava grave with wooden human and bird figures.

Perhaps one of the most eloquent statements of some of the elements involved in such a set of sculptural references occurs in a discussion of Bara ritual by its leading modern interpreter. Sakalava funerary sculpture is yet to be regarded in this light, but some indication of the kinds of concern that might be anticipated may be gauged from Huntingdon's words (1973, p. 82):

> It is not enough to bury someone, merely to dispose of the body. The survivors must bring about a successful conception and rebirth of their deceased kinsman into the world of the ancestors. This process, like the conception of an infant, is a difficult and risky endeavour for both the deceased and his survivors. Should this transition fail, the consequence is nothing short of catastrophic infertility with the deceased remaining like a dead foetus in the womb of his survivors' world.

Amongst the Mahafaly the number of traditional *aloalo* with their naked figures indicated both how the particular deceased was regarded in life and also how intensely rebirth as an ancestor was sought. In modern times, however, these references have disappeared. *Aloalo* are now carved with serious or humorous imagery, often recalling a riot of events which charac-

terised the life of the deceased. The subjects are usually portrayed clothed and the purpose is biographical. *Aloalo* have become obituary announcements when formerly they were notices of rebirth.

The Antanosy in the area of Fort Dauphin and its hinterland have always regarded funerary sculpture as what might be regarded as essentially commemorative. The sites at which the carvings are placed are the cenotaphs, the places of commemoration, where it is customary to erect monuments in stone, cement and wood to each person buried in the communal tomb. Both birds and human figures are reported as appropriate imagery, and certainly there does seem to have been an established tradition of sculpture in the area (although the wet climate in the south-east contributes to a more rapid deterioration of wood sculpture than elsewhere). Indeed, the carver Tsivoloa, who was one of the foremost sculptors of the post Second

Below right Memorial to a man who served with the French authorities and who is also remembered as owning the first motor car in this remote village. The sculptor, Fesira, has shown him seated beside two images recalling these biographical details. Antanosy.

Below Modern figurative carving of a woman developed out of the traditions and subjects of funerary sculpture. Sakalava. H. 98 cm. MAA 63–1–6.

World War period in the Sakalava area was Antanosy by origin (Mallet 1963). Virtually all the sculpture remaining in the Antanosy area at the moment, however, is the work of a single itinerant carver, Fesira.

Most of Fesira's work would seem to date from the immediate pre-war period and includes occasional references to the major local events of the time – the introduction of the first Antanosy-owned motor car in one remote village, or a canoeing accident in another. As with the carvers of the more recent of the *aloalo*, his method of commemoration was not the production of sculpted portraits but of other references to the lives of the deceased. It was not what people looked like but who they were and what they did that made them significant. In practice, however, Fesira's method of work was such that he may well not have known personally those whose cenotaphs he created. He worked on a commission basis, payment being

The top of a memorial which, among other events, commemorates an accident in which a canoe overturned and its occupants drowned. By the Antanosy sculptor Fesira.

made by the descendants of the person commemorated. His practice was to move into the village itself where a house was built in which he would work. Older people recall him as staying for periods from six to nine months, the time it would take to execute the more complicated work. It was the duty of those commissioning him to feed and keep him. They would also relate the events of the life of their dead relative and decide which should be recorded sculpturally; whether it was to be a complex work, or which identifying features should be included if a sole figure – a medallion in the form of a cross, for instance, for the first catechist in a family. Beyond that, however, the conception and execution of the work were the inspiration of Fesira himself.

His sculpture seeks to show its subjects in a conventional light. The figures are carved appropriately clad in pursuit of virtuous tasks or in comfortable repose. Like the portrait painters in the Western tradition who choose to overlook the blemishes of their subject, Fesira consistently presented culturally appropriate images. Who, after all, would wish to commission memorials to their ancestors portrayed otherwise? But, while the eroticism of other sculptural traditions is no part of Antanosy practice, is the purpose and process of creating such a cenotaph purely and simply commemorative?

In documenting Fesira's works and asking in those villages where he had carved about his methods and the circumstances in which he worked, a number of details were constantly related. No one apart from the immediate descendants of the deceased was allowed to see the work while it was being carved. Fesira always worked indoors, in secret. Furthermore, he is often recalled as having worked at night and rested by day. Most strikingly, however, he is reputed to have carved naked. The significance of this is unmistakable: his nakedness reflects the process of conception which the act of carving represents. At another level, however, his nakedness is the prelude to the rebirth of the ancestor commemorated when, for the first time, the finished work is displayed publicly at the cenotaph. The nakedness of the Antanosy *sculptor* recalls the nakedness of the Mahafaly and Sakalava *sculpture*. Fesira was not simply carving memorials but creating ancestors. In that he was heir to the distinctive feature of Malagasy culture practice.

Chronology

The events listed below are largely those discussed in the text, here arranged chronologically for reference.

AD 500 — Approximate date for the first significant settlement of the island.

800–900 — Dates of the first identifiable village sites in the north of the island. Penetration of the interior begins in the south.

1200 — Establishment of Arab settlements. First mosques built.

1500 — 'Discovery' of Madagascar by the Portuguese Diogo Dias. Unsuccessful attempts to establish permanent European bases on the island followed.

1650s — Emergence of Sakalava kingdoms.

Early 1700s — Eastern Madagascar increasingly used as a base by pirates.

1716 — Fénérive captured by Ratsimilao. The beginnings of the Betsimisaraka confederacy.

1750 — Death of Ratsimilao.

1765–1820 — Period of Betsimisaraka and Sakalava raids on the Comores and along parts of the East African coast.

1780 — The future Andrianampoinimerina declared king of Ambohimanga.

1795/6 — Andrianampoinimerina established his capital at Antananarivo.

1810–28 — Radama I, Merina king.

1818 — First mission school opened at Tamatave.

1820 — First mission school opened at Antananarivo.

1828–61 — Ranavalona I, Merina queen.

1835 — Publication of the Bible in Malagasy, but profession of the Christian faith declared illegal.

1836 — Most Europeans and missionaries leave the island.

1861–3 — Radama II, Merina king.

1861 — Missionaries re-admitted. Freedom of religion proclaimed.

1863–8 — Queen Rasoherina succeeds after Radama II assassinated.

1868–83 — Ranavalona II, Merina queen.

1869 — Baptism of Ranavalona II and her husband (the Prime Minister Rainilaiarivony). Destruction of traditional 'idols'.

1883 — Coronation of Queen Ranavalona III.

1895 — Establishment of full French protectorate in Madagascar becoming a colony the following year.

1897 — Ranavalona III exiled first to Réunion and later Algiers. Merina monarchy abolished.

1917 — Death of Ranavalona III in exile.

1938 — Return of the remains of Ranavalona III for reburial in Antananarivo.

1960 — Madagascar achieves full independence.

Bibliography

ABINAL, R. P., 1949–50. 'Le *Fandroana* en Imerina en 1867' *Bulletin de l'Académie Malgache*, XXIX, pp. 20–5

ALTHABE, G., 1969. *Oppression et libération dans l'imaginaire, Les communantés villageoises de la côte orientale de Madagascar*, Maspero, Paris

ANON., 1973. *A Glance at Madagascar*, Tananarive

ARCHER, R., 1976. *Madagascar depuis 1972*, L'Harmattan, Paris

AYACHE, S., 1976. *Raombana l'historien 1809–1855*, Fianarantsoa

BARÉ, J-F., 1976. *Pouvoir des Vivants, language des Morts, idéologiques Sakalave*, Maspero, Paris

BEAUJARD, P., 1983. *Princes et paysans, Les Tanala de l'Ikongo*, L'Harmattan, Paris

BERG, G. M., 1985. 'The sacred musket. Tactics, technology and power in eighteenth century Madagascar', *Comparative Studies in Sociology and History*, 27, 2, pp. 261–79

BERG, G. M., 1986. 'Royal Authority and the Protector System', *Madagascar, Society and History*, ed. C. P. Kottak *et al.*, Carolina Academic Press, Durham, N. Carolina, pp. 175–92

BERNARD-THIERRY, S., 1959. 'Les perles magiques à Madagascar, *Bulletin de la Société des Africanistes*, pp. 33–90

BLOCH, M., 1968. 'Astrology and Writing', *Literacy in Traditional Society*, ed. J. Goody, Cambridge University Press, Cambridge, pp. 277–97

BLOCH, M., 1971. *Placing the Dead, Tombs, Ancestral Villages and Kinship Organisation in Madagascar*, Seminar Press, London

BLOCH, M., 1977a. 'The disconnection between Rank and Power as a process: An outline of the Development of Kingdoms in Central Madagascar', *The Evolution of Social Systems*, ed. J. Friedman and M. Rowlands, Duckworth, London

BLOCH, M., 1977b. 'The past and the present in the present', *Man*, pp. 1321–33.

BLOCH, M., 1981. 'Tombs and States', *Mortality and Immortality*, ed. S. C. Humphreys and H. King, Academic Press, London

BLOCH, M., 1985. 'Almost eating the dead', *Man*, pp. 631–46

BLOCH, M., 1985b. *From Blessing to Violence, History and Ideology in the circumcision ritual of the Merina of Madagascar*, Cambridge University Press, Cambridge

BLOCH, M. (forthcoming). 'The Ritual of the Royal Bath in Madagascar, *Rituals of Royalty, Power and Ceremonial in Traditional Societies*, ed. D. Cannadine and S. R. F. Price, Cambridge University Press, Cambridge

BLOCH, M., and PARRY, J. (eds), 1982. *Death and the Regeneration of Life*, Cambridge University Press, Cambridge

BOUDRY, R., 1933. 'L'Art décoratif Malgache', *La Revue de Madagascar*, pp. 23–83

BOULFROY, N., 1976. 'Vers l'art funéraire mahafaly', *Objets et Mondes*, 16, 3, pp. 95–116

BROWN, M., 1978. *Madagascar Rediscovered*, Damien Tunnacliffe, London

CALLET, R. P., 1873. *Tantaran ny Andriana eto Madagascar*, Tananarive

COLLINS, C., 1898. 'The Fandroana or Annual Festival of the Taimoro', *Antananarivo Annual*, pp. 149–51

COTTE, P. V., 1948. *Regardons vivre une tribu Malgache, Les Betsimisaraka*, Bibliothèque d'Outre-Mer, Paris

COULAUD, D., 1973. *Les Zafimaniry*, Fanontam-Boky Malgasy, Tananarive

DAHL, O., 1951. *Malgache et Maanjan, une comparison linguistique*, Oslo

DECARY, R., 1933. *L'Androy*, Société d'Editions geographiques maritime coloniales, Paris

DECARY, R., 1950. *Moeurs et coutumes des Malgaches*, Payot, Paris

DECARY, R., 1962. *La mort et les coutumes funeraires à Madagascar*, Maisonneuve et Larose, Paris

DECARY, R., 1968. 'L'Art chez les Antandroy', *Civilisation Malgache*, pp. 253–67

DÉLIVRÉ, A., 1974. *L'Histoire des rois d'Imerina*, Klinsiech, Paris

DESCHAMPS, H., 1936. *Les Antaisaka*, Tananarive

DESCHAMPS, H., 1960. *Histoire de Madagascar*, Berger Levrault, Paris

DESCHAMPS, H. and VIANÈS, S., 1959. *Les Malgaches du Sud-Est*, Presses Universitaires de France, Paris

DEZ, J., 1959. 'Chez les Betsimisaraka de la region de Nosy Varika, Les Tangalamena', *Bulletin de la Société des Africanistes*, pp. 299–38

EDMONDS, W. J., 1896a. Bye-gone ornamentation and dress among the Hova Malagasy, *Antananarivo Annual*, pp. 469–77

EDMONDS, W. J., 1896b. 'The Mohara, or war charm of Imerina', *Antananarivo Annual*, pp. 421–5

ELLIS, S., 1985. *The Rising of the Red Shawls, A Revolt in Madagascar 1895–1899*, Cambridge University Press, Cambridge

ELLIS, W., 1838. *History of Madagascar* (2 vols), Fisher, London

ELLIS, W., 1859. *Three visits to Madagascar during 1853–1854–1856*, Murray, London

ELLIS, W., 1867. *Madagascar Revisited*, Murray, London

ESTRADE, J-M., 1977. *Un culte de possession à Madagascar, Le Tromba*, L'Harmattan, Paris

FAUBLÉE, J., 1946. *L'Ethnographie de Madagascar*, Paris

FAUBLÉE, M. U., 1963. *L'Art Malgache*, Presses Universitaires de France, Paris

FAUBLÉE, M. U. and J., 1963. 'Charmes magiques Malgache', *Journal de la Société des Africanistes*, pp. 139–49

FEELEY-HARNIK, G., 1979. 'Construction des monuments funeraires dans la monarchie Behimisatra', *Taloha*, 8, pp. 29–40

FEELEY-HARNIK, G., 1979. 'Divine Kingship and the meaning of history among the Sakalava', *Man*, 13, pp. 402–17

FEELEY-HARNIK, G., 1980. 'The Sakalava House', *Anthropos*, 75, pp. 559–85

FEELEY-HARNIK, G., (forthcoming). 'Clothing and the Organization of Experience', vol. to be pubished by Smithsonian Institution, Washington, D.C.

FERRAND, G., 1908. 'L'Origine Africaine des Malgaches', *Journal Asiatique*, 10, XI, pp. 353–500

FLACOURT, E. DE, 1661. *Histoire de la Grande Isle de Madagascar*, Paris

GENNEP, A. VAN, 1904. *Tabou et Totemisme à Madagascar*, Paris

GRANDIDIER, A., 1891. 'Funeral ceremonies amongst the Malagasy', *Antananarivo Annual*, pp. 304–18

GRANDIDIER, A., 1908. *Ethnographie de Madagascar* (2 vols), Paris

GUERNIER, N. J., 1976. 'Wood sculpting and carving among the Betsileo', *Ethnographie*, 71, pp. 5–22

HARDYMAN, J. T., 1968. 'Notes de Sculpture Sakalava', *Civilisation Malgache*, pp. 269–84

HERTZ, R., 1960 (1907). *Death and the Right Hand*, Cohen and West, London

HEURTEBIZE, G., and RAKOTOARISOA, J. A., 1974. 'Notes sur la confection des tissues de type ikat à Madagascar', *Archipel*, 8, pp. 67–81

HUNTINGDON, W. R., 1973. 'Death and the Social Order, Bara funeral customs', *African Studies*, 32, pp. 65–84

HUNTINGDON, W. R., and METCALF, P., 1979. *Celebration of Death, the anthropology of mortuary ritual*, Cambridge University Press, Cambridge

JOHNSON, H., n.d. *The Living Races of Mankind*, Hutchinson, London

KENT, R., 1970. *Early Kingdoms in Madagascar, 1500–1700*, New York

KENT, R. (ed.), 1979. *Madagascar in History*, Foundation for Malagasy Studies, Albany

KOTTAK, C. P., 1980. *The past in the present, history, ecology, and cultural variation in Highland Madagascar*, University of Michigan Press, Ann Arbor

KOTTAK, C. P., RAKOTOARISOA, J.-A., SOUTHALL, A., VÉRIN, P., 1986. *Madagascar, Society and History*, Carolina Academic Press, Durham, N. Carolina

KUS, S., 1982. 'Matters material and ideal', *Symbolic and Structural Archaeology*, ed. I. Hodder, Cambridge University Press, Cambridge

LAHADY, P., 1979. *Le culte Betsimisaraka*, Ambozontany, Fianarantsoa

LAVONDES, A., 1961. *Art traditionel Malgache*, Tananarive

LOMBARD, J., 1973. 'Les Sakalava-Menabe de la côte Ouest', *Malgache qui est-tu?* Neuchâtel, pp. 89–99

LORIMAN, H., n.d. *L'Art malgache*, Les Arts Coloniaux, Paris

McLEOD, N., 1977. 'Musical instruments and history in Madagascar', *Essays for a Humanist, an offering to Klaus Wachsmann*, Town House Press, New York, pp. 189–215

MALLET, R., 1963. 'Introduction', *Art Sakalava*, Tananarive

MARCUSE, W., 1914. *Through Western Madagascar*, Hurst, London

MICHEL, L., 1957. *Moeurs et coutumes des Bara*, Memoires de l'Académie Malgache, Fasc. XL, Tananarive

MOLET, L., 1952. 'Metiers à tisser Betsimisaraka', *Memoires de l'Institut Scientifique de Madagascar*, 1, 2

MOLET, L., 1956. *Le Bain royal à Madagascar*, Tananarive

MOLET, L, 1979. *La conception malgache du monde du surnaturel et de l'homme en Imerina* (2 vols), L'Harmattan, Paris

MUNTHE, L., 1982. *La tradition arabico-malgache*, Tananarive

OLIVER, S. P., 1866. *Madagascar and the Malagasy*, Day and Son, London

PEYROT, B., 1973. 'Notes sur les steles funéraires en pays Antanosy', *Bulletin de Madagascar*, pp. 277–81

RABEDIMY, J. F., 1976. *Pratiques de divination à Madagascar du sikidy en pays Sakalava-Menabe*, Orstom, Paris

RAHARIJAONA, S., 1962. 'Les pierres levées à Madagascar', *Revue de Madagascar*, 20, pp. 17–30

RAINIVELO, 1875. 'The burning of the idol Ramahavaly', *Antananarivo Annual*, 1, pp. 112–14

RAISON-JOURDE, F. (ed.), 1983. *Les Souverains à Madagascar*, Karthala, Paris

RAOMBANA, 1980. *Histoire, Edition et traduction française par Simon Ayache*, Ambozontany, Fianarantsoa

RICHARDSON, J., 1885. *A new Malagasy-English Dictionary*, London Missionary Society, Antananarivo

ROTH, H. Ling, 1917. *Studies in Primitive Looms*, Halifax

RUUD, J., 1960. *Taboo, a study in Malagasy customs and beliefs*, Allen and Unwin, London

SACHS, C., 1938. *Les instruments de musique de Madagascar*, Institut d'Ethnologie, Paris

SIBREE, J., 1870. *Madagascar and its people. Notes on four years' residence*, Religious Tract Society, London

SIBREE, J., 1880. *The Great African Island*, Trubner, London

SIBREE, J., 1892. 'Decorative carving on wood, especially on burial memorials', *Journal of the Royal Anthropological Society*, XXI, pp. 230–44

SIBREE, J., 1896. *Madagascar before the Conquest*, Fisher Unwin, London

SIBREE, J. (ed.), 1900. 'The Fandroana, or New Year's festival of the Malagasy', *Antananarivo Annual*, 24, pp. 489–96

SIBREE, J., 1915. *A Naturalist in Madagascar*, Seeley, Service and Co. Ltd, London

SOUTHALL, A., 1967. 'The problem of Malagasy Origins', *East Africa and the Orient*, ed. N. Chittick and R. Rotberg, Africana, London

VÉRIN, P., 1964a. 'Les Zafimaniry', *Revue de Madagascar*, 27

VÉRIN, P., 1964b. 'Observations sur les monuments funéraires des Antanosy', *Annales Malgaches*, 3, pp. 47–51.

VÉRIN, P., 1967. 'Austronesian contributions to the culture of Madagascar', *East Africa and the Orient*, N. Chittick and R. Rotberg, Africana, London, pp. 164–91

VÉRIN, P., 1976. 'The African element in Madagascar', *Azania*, pp. 135–51

VÉRIN, P., 1986. *The History of Civilisation in North Madagascar*, Balkema, Rotterdam

VERNIER, J., 1960. *Croyances et coutumes Betsimisaraka*, Paris

VERNIER, J., 1963. 'Bambous gravés malgaches', *Objets et Mondes*, pp. 293–8

VERNIER, J., 1964. 'Etude sur la fabrication des lamba mena', *Journal de la Société des Africanistes*, 34, pp. 7–34

VERNIER, J., 1965. 'Le travail de la canne à Madagascar', *Objets et Mondes*, pp. 21–8

VERNIER, J., 1967. 'Les cannes cérémonielles à Madagascar', *Objets et Mondes*, pp. 247–54

VIG, L., 1969. *Charmes: Spécimens de magie malgache*, Oslo

WEIR, S., 1976. *The Bedouin*, British Museum Publications, London

WILSON, P. J., 1971. 'An ethnographic summary of the Tsimihety of Madagascar', *Behavioural Science Notes*, 6, pp. 33–60

WOULKOFF, M., 1976. 'Notes sur les *aloalo* Mahafaly', *Taloha*, 7, pp. 113–18

Index

References in italic type are to illustrations.